D0539402

Cyberspace

WITHDRAWN FROM STOCK

FOR BEGINNERS

Joanna Buick and Zoran Jevtic

Edited by Richard Appignanesi

LIMERICK
COUNTY LIBRARY
0053+5078

ICON BOOKS

First published in 1995 by Icon Books Ltd.,
52 High Street, Trumpington, Cambridge CB2 2LS

Distributed in the UK, Canada, Europe and Asia by the Penguin Group:
Penguin Books Ltd., 27 Wrights Lane, London W8 5TZ

Published in Australia in 1996 by Allen & Unwin Pty. Ltd.,
PO Box 8500, 9 Atchison Street, St. Leonards, NSW 2065

Text copyright © 1995 Joanna Buick
Illustrations copyright © Zoran Jevtic

The author and artist have their moral rights.

Originating editor: Richard Appignanesi

No part of this book may be reproduced in any form, or by any means,
without prior permission in writing from the publisher.

ISBN 1 874166 24 2

Printed and bound in Great Britain by
The Bath Press, Bath

Cyberspace

cyber from the Greek, *kubernan* - to steer, to guide,
to govern ... to control?

κυβερ *kubernetes... oarsman, steersman*

The word **cyberspace** was first coined by William Gibson in his science fantasy novel **Neuromancer** published in 1984 in which the hero connects a computer directly into his brain ... describing his experience of cyberspace as:

'A graphic representation of data abstracted from the banks of every computer in the human system'.

Norbert Wiener, in 1948, invented the term **cybernetics** to describe control systems using computers. Since then the prefix *cyber* is used in connection with robots and computers, notably the cruel adversaries of the BBCs **Doctor Who** in the 1960s, the Cybermen!

cyberclear

cyberia

cybercome

cybernaut

cyberwill

cybersex

cyberall

cyberotics

cyberfeminism

Other cyber words: **cyberpunk,** a science fiction genre of the 1980s; **cyborg,** a part-human, part-machine resulting from medical advances that incorporates machinery into the body.

As information technologies have advanced towards the scenario presented by Gibson, the word **cyberspace** has come into increasingly common usage, generating more varied definitions and meanings.

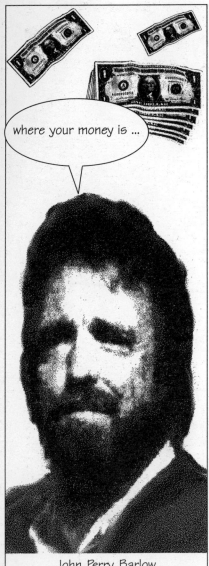

where your money is ...

John Perry Barlow,
Grateful Dead member
and journalist

with electricity we extend our central nervous system globally, instantly interrelating every human experience

predicted by Marshall McLuhan,
the Global Village prophet,
30 years ago

...the only unconquered real estate of the twenty-first century, a virtual world at the electronic frontier inhabited by telematic nomads

Timothy Leary, LSD guru and network advocate

and more prosaically, the network of computer networks and all the information held on it about everything, everywhere...

Cyberspace is then a fortuitous and timely combination of the technologies of **information**, **storage** and **retrieval** with those of global telecommunication

and domestic audiovisual reproduction.

The conjunction of information with networked communication technologies has generated a vast virtual world of knowledge – a parallel universe of recorded data, identification numbers, standards, methods and procedures.

This global pool of information is accessible in theory by everyone.

Banks and multinational corporations have used networked information systems for years. IBM have had their own international 'net' for nearly twenty years!
Wall Street and other major financial institutions worldwide have been consistently on the crest of the technological wave as business has come to rely on speed of transactions and simultaneous communication of prices and deals in the stock markets.
International law enforcement agencies such as Interpol use continent-wide database access to record and assess identification data.

Military and weather satellites transmit data to ground stations around the world to produce extremely detailed information about conditions and activities on the ground.
International air travel has resulted in the constant monitoring and control by an international computer network of thousands of flights every day.
The computer and research departments of separate universities join forces across national boundaries to work together on research projects by connecting and combining their resources by phone lines.

All these technological developments would not have arisen without the human desire to know and communicate.

Language

 People strive to **communicate**. Even with all the paraphernalia of modern technology, saying exactly what you mean can be difficult.

The origins of human language are uncertain.

Gesture was probably the origin of speech, language no doubt connected to tool-making culture – an evolutionary coordination of hand and mind.

Perhaps it happened like this ... sounds uttered involuntarily while gesturing:

The sounds then became names that referred to things as people agreed on them and used them again ...

How language started is less important than appreciating its crucial function: with an agreed vocabulary, things can be shared. Language permits us to share memories, to invent and to imagine the future.

For example, mice and humans have a very similar **DNA** structure, but mice don't have the 'language' that would allow them to discover **DNA**.

All forms of animal life communicate as an essential part of survival. Human language is unique in its capacity for self-reflexive feedback which contributes to cultural adaptation and progress.

Writing

The earliest writing wasn't **alphabetic**, like this, but hieroglyphic. Using simple pictures of common animals and things, the Egyptians recorded stories of the lives of the Pharaohs, their gods, crop reports.

They used 2000 pictographic signs.

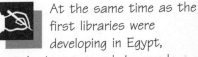

At the same time as the first libraries were developing in Egypt, metal mirrors were being made. This is not entirely irrelevant. The desire to see oneself, to be external to one's own body is a sign of the development of mental life. Writing and self-awareness are facets of human curiosity.

They must also have had ways of recording time, since the first exactly dated year in history occurred in 4241BC, according to the Egyptian calendar.

Around 3500BC, when the first potters' wheels and wheeled vehicles were being used, the first coded language emerged ...

Cuneiform evolved from picture-writing and was read from left to right. The abstracted images still depended on association with the things they originally represented, so it was not truly alphabetical. But it was nevertheless capable of recording poetry, astronomical observations and monetary exchanges.

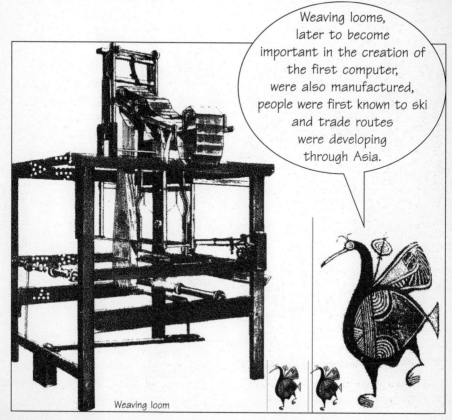

Weaving looms, later to become important in the creation of the first computer, were also manufactured, people were first known to ski and trade routes were developing through Asia.

Weaving loom

Alphabets

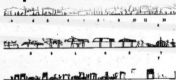

It is thought that Jewish slaves in Sumeria developed the first truly alphabetic written language as a code to communicate without their masters knowing. This Semitic alphabet of 22 signs was derived from the first sound of the name of each hieroglyph in the old system.

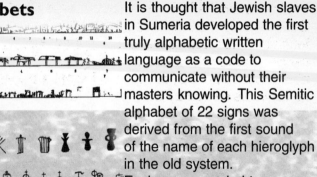

Each corresponded to a consonant and the alphabet contained no vowels, which made it extremely hard to understand – the interpretation of the Talmud has been the subject of debate ever since!

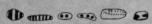

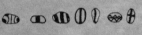

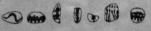

αφδλροπ ωε τφ ϖδλφο
θωερψφι οφοφπ ρε ειοπ
δηφκβ βφι ζχ ∴ξϖμν

The megalithic observatory at Stonehenge was built around this time, bathrooms with a water supply were built in Greece, contraceptives were first used, criminal laws were introduced, the first libraries appeared in Egypt and Pythagoras' system of producing right-angles was used in building.

Moses, hearing the voice of God, received the Word in the form of the Ten Commandments carved into tablets of stone, about 1000 years BC, but their content was carried by word of mouth.

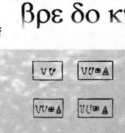

ξτα ψε βιλο
βρε δο κυρ

In this period a Chinese dictionary of 40,000 characters was produced, the epic of Gilgamesh was first recorded, the first attempt was made to build a canal at Suez, the first labour strikes took place and regulations were introduced on beer.

As one explores historical records, it becomes apparent that whatever major technical developments were taking place in whichever part of the world, people were learning to communicate more efficiently, were expressing themselves, enjoying themselves and making their presence felt in ways that are still used today!

Dream-time

 The earliest forms of mass communication were public meetings (for example, Christ speaking to a crowd of 4000 people) and theatre. Early Greek drama was performed outdoors for audiences of up to 30,000 people – all without amplification!

Shared imagination also found expression in mysticism and ritual. Collective tribal dreaming is a characteristic of Native American and Australian Aboriginal peoples who believe individual waking life is a shadow of the rich and infinite dreamworld.

Human beings have always used technology to enhance communication and feel part of something greater and more meaningful than they experience alone – the belief in a collective unconscious, or at least a shared dream, doesn't go away.

And as the manufacturing methods of the Industrial Revolution demonstrated, there are ways in which a collection of methods and machines is greater than the sum of its parts.

The importance of ritual in making people feel connected has long been known. The trance states brought on by the dancing dervishes, by incantation and by hallucinogenic foods have all served to draw groups of people together and give them a common identity.

News Travels

From 1000BC onwards, languages and libraries proliferated, schools and academies appeared in stable civilizations, and stories and plays were recorded.

Homer, Aesop, Buddha and Confucius all lived in this millennium.
The first Olympic games were held.
Library documents from the Assyrian capital Nineveh show transactions of sale, exchange, rental, loan interest and mortgages...

Long before the mass media news networks, a succession of powerful empires, from China to ancient Sumer and Egypt to Rome, created land and sea routes along which information of all sorts was swiftly conveyed – military dispatches, stories of new lands, strange animals, unusual food ...

Around 2000BC, when Eratosthenes first suggested that the Earth moved round the Sun, slaves were being sold in Rome, the Venus de Milo was carved, a slave of Cicero invented a system of shorthand and the first college of technology was started near the famous library at Alexandria.

THE MEANS OF COMMUNICATION

rapidly increased as cultures came into contact through imperial and trade expansion.

Increased contact spread
THE PLAGUE

and from AD 547 to 594 the population of Europe was halved – every silver lining has a cloud.

SCROLLS

began to be replaced by books. Map-making and astronomy became widespread. Algebra, powers and roots of numbers, decimal reckoning were known throughout Asia and Europe.

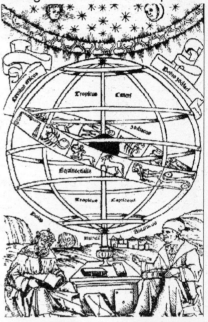

THE BIBLE

In AD 600, Pope Gregory ruled that 'pictures were books for illiterates', and they could spread the message of the Bible more widely.

While in Europe books were still being written by hand in monasteries, in China, nearly 800 years before Gutenberg, books were being printed ...

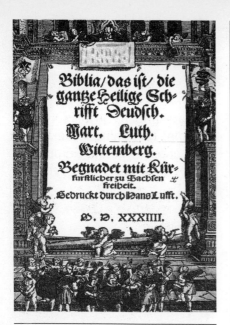

NEWS SERVICE IN AD 650

In AD 650 the Caliphs introduced the first organized news service, the first Indian dictionary and romantic novels were produced, Muhammad's teachings were collected into the book called the Koran, and notation in music began.

An illustrated page from the Koran

MECCA

In AD 628 Muhammad came to Mecca and wrote letters to all the rulers of the world, so beginning the first religion based on the written word ...

POWER

for milling was commonly produced by water wheels, and the weaving of cloth was by now universal ...

NEWSPAPER

The first printed newspaper was published in Beijing and St. Vitus' dance (chorea disease) became epidemic across Europe.

LIMERICK
COUNTY LIBRARY

Learning, libraries and literature

 The evolution of tool-making, followed by the development of language and writing, gave us the possibility of abstraction, memory and storage of information.

In ancient times written information, being rare and often sacred, was accumulated, forming libraries.
Around 1000BC there was a Hittite library in 8 languages. Maps and histories became emblems of empire for incumbent rulers – and were destroyed by conquering armies in early support of the notion that **knowledge is power**.

To produce Ptolemy's 10 volume guide to Greece in AD 170 required security and peace, as did the complete encyclopedia of Isidore of Seville in AD 622, and a 1000 volume Chinese encyclopedia in AD 984.

Great libraries were both political and commercial assets, storing and selling information and providing writing and book-copying services. They were also the basis of the first schools – for boys and men. In 105BC the library at Alexandria had hosted the first college of technology.

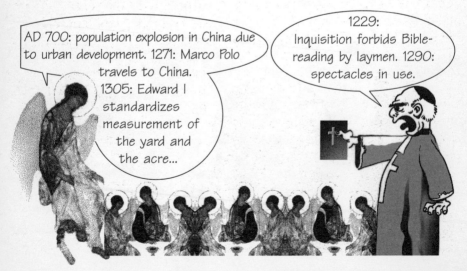

AD 700: population explosion in China due to urban development. 1271: Marco Polo travels to China. 1305: Edward I standardizes measurement of the yard and the acre...

1229: Inquisition forbids Bible-reading by laymen. 1290: spectacles in use.

As civilization spread, messengers were sent further afield in shorter times. Horse-changing posts were introduced in France in AD 797 and by AD 942 the Persian empire had 1000 stations for its postal and news service.

Static electricity had been known in ancient Greece, its principles used today in the photocopying process.

Magnetism had been used in compasses to find North as early as AD 271 in China.

Petrol (gasoline), called 'burning water' was discovered by the Japanese in AD 615.

Zero was incorporated in Arabic numerals in AD 814 and its importance recognized in AD 1000.

Around the same year, the Chinese discovered gunpowder and the eternal human dream of flight was seen in drawings of designs for flying machines.

Homer's **Iliad** and **Odyssey** had been written down around 900BC. Over the next thousand years, people worldwide recorded histories in drama, song and story. Travelling musicians carried news between all parts of the 'known world'. In India, a romantic novel was published in AD 650.

Homer

illuminated manuscript

Madness and exploration

Exploration had been a by-product of trade and war, involving journeys into jungles and deserts, seeking new resources and finding new markets.

In AD 1492, after Martin Behaim had constructed the first terrestrial globe, Christopher Columbus set out to discover the westward route to India.

Christopher Columbus

As European culture and scholarship became standardized, **madness** was invented.

Before urbanization and the social concepts of acceptable behaviour and conformity became common, people of all varieties lived in small rural communities, all their time taken up in survival.

In urban centres, 'deviant' behaviour was more easily noticed and punished.

> Just as merchants
> with mutual interests gathered
> at trade fairs in Europe as early as 1300,
> fools and lunatics began to be identified
> and segregated.

Joan of Arc

'Bedlam' Hospital was opened in London in 1407, Joan of Arc was burned at the stake.

In1494 Sebastian Brant published **Das Narrenschiff** – Ship of Fools.
Boats were sent down the Rhine from one town to the next, carrying mad people unwanted in their home communities.

These wandering fools were thus a symptom of the narrowing of 'normal' behaviour, their experience and knowledge denied value, in the same way as heretics.

Questions of access to information, the decisions about which knowledge is valuable and which expendable start here. So began the exploration and mapping of the human psyche, possibly the last frontier to be traversed by humankind, as Columbus discovered the New World.

Building cyberspace

 Cyberspace is the greatest 'sum' so far created by human beings.

The mystical and all-encompassing vocabulary of 'cyberia' and the 'internet' is symptomatic of the participants desire to create a utopian world of total knowledge, a human-made machine with all the answers ...

Before we consider whether or not those aims are achievable or desirable, it is useful to look at how technology came into existence and how it works.

The following pages will explain and de-mystify some of the basic technologies necessary to computing, telecommunication and image -processing.

This approach is intended to show how standards and formats that we take for granted came into existence, and enable the fledgling cybernaut to engage with and even speak about the technologies of cyberspace in an informed and relaxed way!

First some definitions...
Data are facts, numbers, assertions...
(one datum is...)

Will the vast electronic library of cyberspace generate wisdom? Or will browsing haphazardly through oceans of facts and opinions merely produce passive consumers of data, bringing scholarship to an end?

Information
is data processed into a form that is meaningful...
The application and analysis of information through
discipline and experience produce knowledge.

Information
Technology (IT),
the bedrock of
cyberspace, can be
defined as the creation,
collection, storage,
processing, transmission,
display and use of
information by people
and things.
(Open University
definition)

If you wanted to create
cyberspace from scratch, what
would you need?
-systematized information
-education
-writing and visual
communication
-ways of sending and receiving
information
-electricity
-machines for handling huge
quantities of information
-storage systems...

You would
also need political will,
commercial investment
and development, and
cultural desire.

But first ...
the history of technology, making
cyberspace possible.

(Remember, history isn't orderly, so inventions
and knowledge often arrive earlier or later than
you might expect, and like the weather it
varies in different parts of the world.)

SHOCK! HORROR!
GUTENBERG
BEGINS PRINT REVOLUTION
IN GERMANY IN 1450

There were too many characters in Eastern written languages to make this system viable in the East.

Gutenberg's original type was similar to Gothic script, but was replaced by a Roman typeface in 1470. This was specially designed for the printing process and was easier to read.

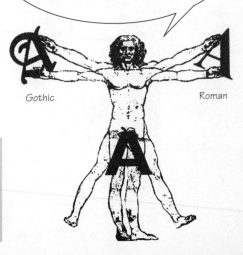

Gothic   Roman

Although a book using movable type had been printed in Korea in 1409, Johannes Gutenberg of Mainz is credited with starting the new age of communication in the 15th century.

Moveable type (a printing block for each page cast from a hand-assembled set of individual reversed letters) meant that any number of copies of those pages could be printed.

Information storage and retrieval.
Gutenberg's first publication was the
Bible, 1282 pages in 2 volumes.

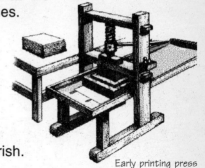

Although only a few hundred copies
were printed, of which 38 survive
today, it is easy to imagine that
papermaking would become a
lucrative business, that mass
production would create a publishing
industry and that libraries would flourish.

Early printing press

1403: 22,937 volume Chinese
encyclopedia, 3 copies made.

Education
Books from all over Europe
were now available in Latin and
Greek, the standard languages
of learning, encouraging a
uniformity in education and
culture across Europe.

Communications
Standardization in European
languages of left to right script,
partly because of the introduction
of conventions in typesetting.

I invented the
parachute in 1480
I wrote both left to right
and right to left!

Leonardo da Vinci

Computing
Nothing much yet!

Entertainment
Bibles and dictionaries were the
breadwinning publications in the
early days of printing, but were
soon followed by legal texts, Latin
and Greek classics and
eventually manuals of etiquette,
hygiene, travel and poetry.

29

Numbers

- Decimal numerals were in use in Crete as early as 1500BC.

- The height of the sun was calculated in China before the birth of Christ.

- The first book of algebra was written by Diophantus in Alexandria in AD 250.

Numbers were believed to contain truth, and magic squares and other mathematical puzzles were regarded as the domain of philosophy.

Arabic numerals were used in Baghdad in AD 760 and Euclid's geometry was translated into Arabic. Islam forbade representation of human or natural forms, resulting in an abstract art of mathematical patterns and arabesques.

Devotion to abstract concepts gave the Arab world a distinct advantage in mathematical progress and they introduced arithmetical notation to Europe.

The Hindu astronomer Aryabhata first considered the powers and roots of numbers in circa AD 500, and then began using the decimal number system.

Powers :
2 to the power 2, written as 2^2, means 2×2 and is equal to 4; 2^3 is therefore $2 \times 2 \times 2 = 8$ and 3^5 is $3 \times 3 \times 3 \times 3 \times 3 = 243$.

Roots work the other way: the square root of 4 is 2; since $2 \times 2 = 4$.
The cube root of 27 is 3, since $3 \times 3 \times 3 = 27$.

$2 \times 2 = 4$

$3 \times 3 = 9$

650 notation in music
870 calibrated candles for time-keeping
980 organ with 400 pipes at Winchester monastery- a feat of control engineering
1050 time value given to notes in music
1071 Papal 'world' dominance
1309 counterpoint in music
1322 Pope forbids counterpoint
1347-1351 Black death in Europe - 75 million people die
1414 Financial centres in Florence lead to the Medici becoming bankers to the Papacy
1494 Luca Pacioli - cubic equations
German lottery - 'Pots of Luck'!

> Why all these **dates**?

1504 The earliest surviving pocket watch, the 'Nuremberg Egg' made by P. Henlein. Awareness of time passing had started.
1519 Magellan circumnavigating the world
1523 Dürer produces the first German geometry manual
1530 Frisius calculates longitude by difference in times, impossible before the invention of a portable, reliable clock
1563 Plague in Europe and, as a result of infection by European explorers, 2 million South American Indians die of typhoid circa 1567
1576 decimal fractions invented by Viete in France
1589 Reverend William Lee builds the first knitting machine, a stocking frame, but has to take it to France because Elizabeth I will not allow hand-knitters to be made redundant by its introduction
1590 First paper mill in England

1591 use of letters for quantities in algebra
1595 A catalogue of English printed books published
1596 ratio of diameter to circumference of circle - π
1600, The philosopher **Giordano Bruno** burned at the stake in Rome for heretical belief in Copernican astronomy
William Gilbert, physician to Elizabeth I, publishes a treatise on **magnetism and electricity deducing that the Earth's magnetic field behaves as if there is a huge magnet between the poles**
1615 Galileo faces Inquisition

> They are only a small sample of **everything**!

1623 Patents law in England
1629 Albert Gerard uses brackets in calculation – a step towards logic
1631 William Oughtred proposes the uses of **x as the sign for multiplication**
1635 Speed limit introduced for hackney coaches in London – of 3mph!
1637 prohibition of foreign books in Japan
1639 First printing press in North America, in Cambridge, Massachusetts
1642 Puritans close all theatres in England
1643 Parcel post in France and library book loan on subscription in Austria

For **anything** to happen in history, **everything** has to be in place. Cyberspace is a sum of everything past ... and still to come.

Clocks

Increasing speed of communication introduced new concepts of time ...

Chinese water clock

Egyptian water clock

Mr John Harrison of Barrow-upon-Humber after 40 years succeeded in 1761 in producing a device only 5 ¼" wide, accurate to half a minute per year and adjustable for varying temperatures. This was the first opportunity for sailors to experience how far they were from home in **time** as well as in **space**.

Galileo

At first, it took so long to travel across continents that days and nights were assumed to occur at the same time in all places.

Church bells were rung five times a day as a call to prayer, long before they told the time, (an example of secularization in religion, an appeal to an absolute apart from God).

By 1389 the bells of Rouen Cathedral were being rung every quarter of an hour.

Since longitudinal position was calculated by time, it was important that ships' clocks were accurate.

In 1714 the British Parliament offered a reward of £20,000 (a huge fortune in those days) for an accurate timepiece.

J. Harrison's clock

 In Paris, in 1880, the Curie brothers noticed that crystals vibrate at a constant frequency when a voltage is applied to them, and that, conversely, an electric charge is produced when a crystal is bent or hit. This phenomenon, called the piezo-electric effect, was first used to keep time in 1929 – the vibrations of a quartz crystal were counted electronically and used to control an electric motor.

The speed of the vibration of the crystal depends on keeping the temperature steady – the resulting clock can be extremely accurate.

The concept of the Earth as a sphere moving round the Sun took time to be introduced and accepted. Galileo was accused of blasphemy for so doing. Ordinary people's experience of the Earth as a **globe** arrived with mass air travel and international telephone calls.

Hoy, Galileo! The Earth is still flat!

Interesting times ...

As information and ideas spread across the world, as armies and merchants travelled further afield, so too did disease, mass plagues and then syphilis circa 1498.

The dissemination of knowledge through the printed book was also thought to be dangerous ...

1514: pineapples arrive in Europe...

1519: Luther says "Bull!" to Pope.

1515: printing of books banned unless permitted by the Roman Catholic authorities!

1529: first manual on alchemy published!

Luther's questioning of Papal infallibility in 1519 and his subsequent burning of a Papal Bull in 1520 were significant both for their publicity and the symbolic destruction of the printed text: don't believe everything you read!

Luther

1500: Aldus Manutius *invented italics;* Lead pencils used in England; Regular post between Vienna and Brussels; 1503: invention of pocket handkerchief. 1512: I claimed that the Earth goes round the Sun.

Copernicus

Utopian idealism and the quest for ultimate truth and the elixir of life had been the dream of many scholars since the Academy at Athens, 2000 years previously, and the birth of alchemy around AD 400. The idea of a **single unifying theory** began here and has never gone away.

Individual scholars, sharing their ideas through the distribution of texts, believed that increased access to information would inevitably lead to the knowledge of everything.

They certainly believed that gold could be made from base metals, such as lead, if they could only say the right words in the right order.

Many books of spells and alchemical incantations (the basis of modern chemistry) were published. In 1546 attempts were made to find El Dorado, the fabled golden city of the Incas in Venezuela, and in 1547 Nostradamus made his long-term prophecies.

Nostradamus

Incas sculptures

Incredible shrinking world

Early holidays were holy days... and excursions abroad nearly always had commercial, military or religious reasons.

Only the rich could afford to travel, usually in the pursuit of health or education.

The Grand Tour became an essential part of a young aristocrat's preparation for life, a duty for self-improvement. The increasingly wealthy merchant classes aspired to this lifestyle, and spas were developed closer to home, resulting eventually in trips to the seaside and 'to take the air'.

Salt water was accepted by physicians as being as good for the constitution as the rarer and more expensive mineral spas.

In the early 1800s, wooden steamboats plied between London and the Kent coast on the 8-hour journey to Margate and Ramsgate, a huge reduction in the time taken for the same journey by carriage on the roads.

In 1812, 17,000 passengers

and by 1820, 98,000 passengers...

The Industrial Revolution transformed both people's lives and the towns and cities to which they increasingly moved to find work.

Agriculture was unable to sustain the burgeoning populations of Europe. The aspirations of European and American citizens were changing, along with their countries' economies.

Steam engine

Factories provided steady employment all year round and cheap train travel led to migration of workers to industrial centres – suburbia was born, and with it, the commuter.

The speed and low fares of travel by steamship increased emigration to the New Worlds.

Most workers lived in tied accommodation and were paid in kind with food or fuel rather than money.

The new **working class** (a term not yet coined) was employed in factories and paid a weekly wage, for long hours and no paid holiday. It was, however, *just* possible for some people to save a little money and to choose what to spend it on.

'Disposable income' meant the start of consumerism, recreation, leisure time and the acceleration of fashion.

Emigration to colonies meant that correspondence between friends and relatives became common.

 Literacy increased parallel with the proliferation of newspapers, especially sensational Sunday papers. Up-to-date national and international newspapers and the post were made possible by the improving railway services.

'Common knowledge' took on a new meaning as the whole world began to read the same news – finance, disasters and of course weather ...

The Penny Post started in Britain in 1840. And in almost every railway station there was a bookstall!
It is estimated that the railways doubled the number of books printed and published.

Thomas Cook's first charter excursion in 1841 between Leicester and Loughborough was to a temperance meeting. Thus began Cook's excursion into package tours both in Britain and overseas.

We led a Grand Tour of Europe for paying customers in 1856. My company expanded during the 1860s to become a ticket agency for international travel and also distributed post abroad.

Thomas Cook

Yes!

This period saw a huge increase in travel, both physically, and mentally through letter-writing, the picture postcard, newspaper reports and the rise of fiction.

The 19th century novel ranged in subject matter from romantic and domestic stories and sea-faring adventures...

... to the fantastical journeys of Jules Verne (**Two Thousand Leagues under the Sea**), and my very own **Frankenstein!**

Jules Verne

Mary Shelley

The invention of popular culture ...

 Circuses and fairgrounds vied with each other to produce the most shocking and memorable spectacles.

Music halls and popular songs made stars out of the favourite performers.

People started to think about their appearance, not only in terms of fashionable costume, but also about their bodies. Self-consciousness had truly arrived.

The gap between rich and poor widened considerably during the Industrial Revolution.
The British Empire was built on mechanization and the imposition of commercial terms, believed to be 'fair and generous'.

Divisions of rank and status as rigid as the Hindu caste system ensured normative social codes of practice ... a place for everything and everything in its place.

... and museums

Those with a wanderlust became explorers, financing expeditions of discovery and starting a trend for the collection of souvenirs.

Great museums appeared in European cities, such as the Pitt-Rivers Museum in Oxford, England, showing a startlingly eclectic display seemingly organized by purpose.

The discoveries of explorers and collectors were catalogued in libraries. Systems for organizing knowledge grew to accommodate the expanding range of subjects and their specialisms.
John Dewey's decimal classification system, first used in 1876, is still in use in many public libraries today.

Information poured out of experts, while diaries and leisure-time hobbies became popular.
And of course, as the railways arrived, so too did the train-spotter!

Algebra

 The word algebra comes from 'al-jabr' used by Muhammad ibn-Musa al-Khwarizmi, an Arab who lived and worked in Baghdad in the 9th century. Modern physics relies almost entirely upon mathematical discovery through algebra.

The language of mathematics is a common language for people who can't speak to each other!
Although a lot of maths was developed before algebraic signs were invented, modern notation is now universal.

π is 3.14159265358979323846....

$$\{(1\underset{1514}{+}1\underset{1631}{-}1) \underset{}{\times} \{1\underset{1659}{\div}1\}\} \underset{1557}{=} 1$$

Other symbols include the use of (brackets)[]{} of all shapes ...
S for sum. Leibniz's notation for calculus (dy/ dx) was adopted in the 19th century.

$$\zeta \; \gamma \; \beta \; \varepsilon \; \rho \; \delta \; \pi \; \alpha \; \zeta \; \varepsilon$$

We are all more familiar with algebraic notation than we imagine.

gross income is: £G
tax free allowance: £g
tax rate: x%
then net income: N
= g + (G−g)(100−x)

$$\sum 5! = 5+4+3+2+1$$

42

The abacus

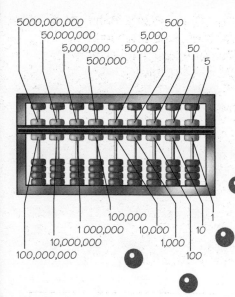

5000,000,000
50,000,000
5,000,000
500,000

500
5,000
50,000

50
5

100,000
1 000,000   10,000
10,000,000   1,000
100,000,000

1
10
100

The abacus developed from a system of calculation using pebbles and shells to represent numbers into an arrangement of fixed rods carrying beads.

Used by merchants in China for thousands of years, its speed and accuracy made it universally popular. As systems of bartering were replaced by currency exchange, assessment of worth and value became essential. The abacus is still used on a daily basis in some parts of the Far East, where pocket calculators or batteries to run them are too expensive.

Business

Financial calculation of taxes, profits and losses became immense as large-scale industry developed in the 19th century. Huge numbers of clerical workers were employed by banks and businesses, and bureaucracy was born.

Small mechanical calculators were widely used towards the end of the nineteenth century. These machines were only capable of simple arithmetic. Although these calculators increased the clerks' speed of working, the volume of numerical calculation was also increasing enormously.

Electricity changed the machines, but the human effort needed to feed in data and control the computers did not diminish.

Pascal's calculator

Blaise Pascal, mathematician and philosopher, built a mechanical calculator using a system of cogged wheels and ratchets when he was 19 years old. It took several years to construct and was made to help his father, a tax collector. It was unreliable and expensive, though beautifully made, and he only sold about 15 of them.

L' AMAZING CALCULATING MACHINE

with simple owner's manual for beginners and professionals written by the inventor himself!

ORDER NOW TO AVOID DISAPPOINTMENT!

IDEAL GIFT!

Copyright by B. Pascal, All rights reserved

The principles of mechanical calculation remained the same until Jacquard introduced the idea of externally supplied data on punched cards.

The first (nearly) computer

In 1804, at the Paris Conservatoire des Arts et Métiers' Joseph Marie Jacquard, a textile  manufacturer, invented a method of controlling the warp threads on a carpet loom using the first 'programme'.

A series of cards with holes punched in them, later joined to form an endless loop, determined which threads would be raised and lowered when the shuttle passed between them, thus establishing the pattern on the carpet.

While assisting John Herschel (astronomer and the inventor of sensitized photographic paper) with astronomical  calculations in 1830, Charles Babbage (1801-1871) became interested in the possibility of making a 'difference engine' to perform complex mathematical calculations.

The machine was for finding the differences between the values of variables in equations. Babbage designed it so that having set the first value correctly it would produce thousands of results without error. This machine was not completed, but he persisted with an 'analytical engine' based on Jacquard's punched cards. The cards would input the information, store and print results. He didn't finish this one either.

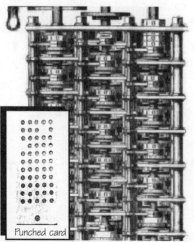

Punched card

Charles Babbage and his difference engine

45

Electricity and electromagnetism

The word electricity derives from the Greek word for amber which was known as early as 500 BC to acquire an electric charge when rubbed, attracting feathers and hair. All matter is made of atoms which have a positively charged nucleus surrounded by electrons which have negative charges.

Atoms normally like to have equal numbers of electrons and protons, so that their overall charge is balanced at zero. If an electron gets knocked away from its atom, there are then more protons than electrons and the overall charge on the atom is positive. This is called **static electricity**.

Normal

Positive

If atoms with extra electrons (i.e. negatively charged) are connected to a positively charged atom, electrons will move between them to try and balance the charges in all the atoms. On a large scale, with lots of electrons flowing from one place to another, this is called an electric current.

This difference in charges is measured in volts, after the Italian Alessandro Volta who discovered the phenomenon in 1800. The flow of current produces heat and light.

In 1820, Oersted observed that a current flowing in a wire produced a magnetic field around it, causing a magnetized needle to move in proportion to the amount of current flowing, which could then be measured. Current is measured in amps, named after Monsieur Ampère, whose work made the electric telegraph possible.

Ampère

Michael Faraday

In 1831 I experimented with the opposite idea and found that moving a wire in a magnetic field caused a current to flow in the wire.

Faraday's discovery led to the building of the first dynamo and was the beginning of the modern era. I developed the idea to produce alternating current electricity, which proved far more effective than direct current, the kind batteries produce which moves in one direction only.

Nikola Tesla

 Alternating current (AC) supplies far more current than direct current (DC) and is generated for our homes by any machine that can turn a magnet around a wire, such as water-wheels, steam and fuelled engines.

The theoretical relationship between electricity and magnetism was formulated by J.C. Maxwell between 1855 and 1864. He was the first to suggest the possibility of radio waves.

Heinrich Hertz continued his work and confirmed the existence of radio waves in 1888. The frequency of electromagnetic waves is named after him.

Hertz

Hang on eine minuten! Vot iz frequency? And vot does light have to do with ze radio?

Okay, a wave looks like this...

⊢1 cycle⊣

and the number of times it repeats itself, a cycle, each second is called the frequency:
1 kilohertz = 1,000 cycles per sec.

Telegraph

From smoke signals, bonfires and beacons at the time of the Roman Empire to more sophisticated systems using flags and semaphore, messages have been transmitted using simple codes.

Electric telegraphy by wire was a possibility first suggested as early as 1753 in Scotland, and messages were actually sent one kilometre by Francisco Salva of Barcelona in 1804 using a battery-powered system in which each letter used a separate wire.

Although important documents had to be physically moved from place to place, secret information was signalled through private codes as it is today.

The international telegraph network began with the laying of cables across the English Channel in 1851. By 1866, transatlantic cables, first laid by Brunel from his steamship **Great Eastern** in 1858, were used by Julius Reuter, founder of the German news agency.

In 1855, the original single contact signalling mechanism was replaced by a keyboard that sent electric signals corresponding to each letter and printed out at the receiving end.

Morse code for SOS

Q: Here come dots (anagram of) A: The Morse Code.

Transferring messages on to a punched tape made possible the transmission of up to 100 words per minute.

The number of units of signal per minute that can be sent over a line is called the baud rate, named after Emile Baudot who developed a technique for sending several signals simultaneously along one wire, called multiplexing.
multiplexing.
multiplexing.
multiplexing.
multiplexing.
multiplexing.

Mechanized transmission of telegraph messages from keyboards became known as teletype, then telex, and at its peak employed thousands of operators sending messages between small towns throughout the USA and Europe.

In 1838 I patented a simple coding system which depended on the duration of the signal rather than its amplitude.
Morse code is still in use towards the end of the 20th century and is the basis of digital transmission.
At first up to ten words per minute could be transmitted or transcribed by an experienced operator.

Samuel Morse

Telephone

The telephone was invented by Alexander Graham Bell in 1876.
Researching methods of teaching deaf people to speak, he built the first microphone using a vibrating reed which converts the sound waves of speech into the physical movements of an electromagnet to produce electric signals which are sent along wires to another transducer containing a reed that reproduces the original sound.

Early telephones had only one transducer for both listening and speaking until Edison produced a system with two.

Until the 1950s, it was common for these to be separate, unlike the ergonomically designed handset we all recognize.

To promote his invention, Bell campaigned in Europe and the USA, even demonstrating the telephone to Queen Victoria in 1878.

Send reinforcements, we're going to advance!

In a **WW1** anecdote, a message sent from the front line to the supporting units became unrecognizable.

The telephone was considered a novelty at first and was rejected by the British Post Office representative on the grounds that although America might enjoy such gimmicks, London had enough small boys to run messages...

My dear Edison, why not suggest to Mr Bell that he develop a more ergonomical model...

As the phone network grew, the number of operators required to connect callers increased enormously, until the invention of an automatic telephone exchange by a Kansas undertaker. Almon Strowger discovered that the exchange operator was connecting calls intended for him to her boyfriend, his rival, who was taking all his business. The automatic telephone exchange is now very sophisticated, handling many calls simultaneously.

Every aspect of life has become dependent on the telephone network, from private conversations and business calls and faxes, to international governmental communication and connection to the computer communications system known as the **Internet** ... about which more later.

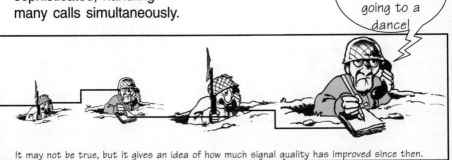

Send three – and – fourpence, we're going to a dance!

It may not be true, but it gives an idea of how much signal quality has improved since then.

Photography ...

How do we see things?

Cameras receive light just as the human eye does, a lens providing a way of focusing the incoming light, and the aperture of the camera, working as the iris does in changing the size of the pupil, controlling how much light reaches the film.

Arab astronomers used the principle of the camera to observe the Sun.

Far too bright to look at with the naked eye, sunspots and eclipses could be viewed on the floor of a room with a small aperture in the ceiling, now called a 'camera obscura', Latin for 'dark room'.

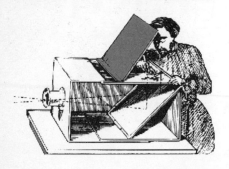

The development of the modern camera required a lens system to focus light and the invention of film on which to record it.

In 1841 Fox-Talbot developed the calotype process using transparent film from which multiple prints could be made.

The detail of the scene recorded in the image is at the scale of the chemical crystals, which is very small indeed!

52

...and Holography

A holograph is a three-dimensional photograph using a laser beam of pure, coherent light split into a reference beam which shines directly at the glass photographic plate and another which illuminates the object being photographed.

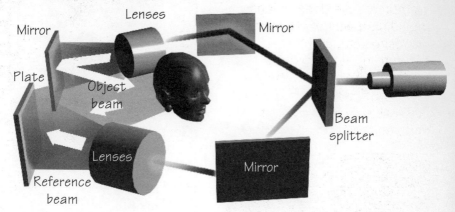

The size and curvature of the photographic plate determines the three-dimensional holographic range of the image – the larger the plate, the more 3D there is.

A simple way to think about it is that a holographic plate will allow about as much variance of position as a window of a similar size showing the same scene. So a big window curved around an object will show more aspects of it and the image will be more three-dimensional.

When a hologram is broken, the image is not. A fragment of the original will still show the whole scene but with less 3 dimensionality, as though through a smaller window.

Film

Eadweard Muybridge had experimented with sequences of photographs taken at short intervals to see how horses' legs really moved, and Etienne Marey produced the first film rolls on paper.

Techniques to give the audience a more enveloping experience were first used in **'The Jazz Singer'** (**sound**) in 1927; a **Technicolour** Disney cartoon in 1932; **widescreen** Cinerama in 1952; **3D** using red-green spectacles in 1953!

George Eastman, founder of Kodak, introduced a celluloid base so that the images became transparent, making projection possible.

Frankly, my dear, I don't give a damn!

The Imax system uses
70mm film projected onto
a huge curved screen.
The audience sits close to the
screen which fills their vision.
In some cinemas the seats
are motorized, moving in
sync with the film!

Videofilm has become a format
in its own right.
The next stage, after CD and
video disc games, is 3D
interactive Virtual Reality.

The film is stopped for a fraction of a second as each photograph is taken separately. The standard film speed is 24 pictures per second. The projector stops the film at each frame to project it. Hence the characteristic purring sound of cine-projectors as they stop and start every 24th of a second.

But what about computers?

Computers work by manipulating numbers– they don't 'understand' anything other than zeros and ones fed into microprocessors and electronic components in the form of changes in voltage, normally 5 volts for 1 and 0 volts for 0.
The computer 'looks' at a series of voltage pulses representing binary numbers and uses extremely simple logic to deal with it.

The decisions that the computer makes are based on symbolic logic developed by George Boole, a British mathematician and published as the *Mathematical Analysis of Logic* in 1847.

Boole's work followed on from logic diagrams of Ramon Lull, a 13th century mystic from Majorca, and was succeeded by the diagrammatic extension of the syllogism, the Venn diagram, named after John Venn.

Boolean algebra depends on electrical signals being 'present' (1) or 'not present' (0). This is a binary system using only two symbols to represent everything!

The actual voltages involved in the devices which perform the Boolean functions are irrelevant. What counts is whether the signal is there (1) or not there (0).

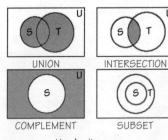

Venn's diagrams

Computing decisions are based on Boolean algebra and involve comparing two pieces of data and using the logic operators AND, OR and NOT to determine what to do next.

Boole

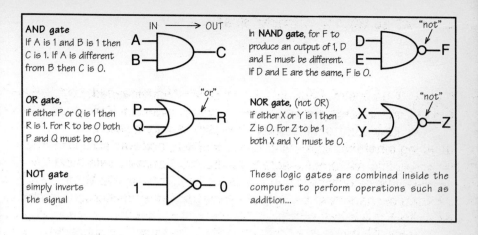

AND gate
If A is 1 and B is 1 then C is 1. If A is different from B then C is 0.

In **NAND gate**, for F to produce an output of 1, D and E must be different. If D and E are the same, F is 0.

OR gate,
if either P or Q is 1 then R is 1. For R to be 0 both P and Q must be 0.

NOR gate, (not OR) if either X or Y is 1 then Z is 0. For Z to be 1 both X and Y must be 0.

NOT gate
simply inverts the signal

These logic gates are combined inside the computer to perform operations such as addition...

and this is what is actually happening inside the machine:

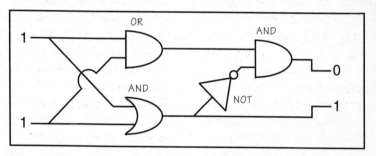

This simple logic, when applied many times to binary numbers in particular and controlled ways, can result in the most complex calculations – everything that digital computers do can be reduced to these simple functions. To carry out these logic comparisons using electricity required the invention of the thermionic valve.

The case of AND gate where the same type produces output.

In case of NAND gate, different types produce output.

Valves & audio

Edison

Wow!
This gotta be named after me...

A current flowing from positive to negative means electrons flowing from negative to positive. In the thermionic valve this current can be altered by applying a small current to the grid. By controlling this small current to produce variations in the larger current, it becomes possible to make the large current vary in the same way as the small one.

This is called **amplification** and is the basis of early radio and audio technology.

In 1897, J. J. Thomson discovered the flow of electrons from a filament to a positively charged electrode and named it the Edison effect. With this property of electron flow, the study of electricity branched out into **electronics**.

The first thermionic (from the Greek word 'therme' for heat) triode valve was built and patented in 1906 by an American engineer, Lee de Forest. This was the first electronic mechanism capable of comparing two inputs to produce a logical output, making the application of Boolean algebra possible.

Wrong!
I'll show you amplification basis!

The introduction of amplification made long-distance calls possible and made radio transmissions stronger and their reception better, as a weak signal could be amplified at the receiver.

In 1877, Edison made the first replayable recording.

He used a steel stylus which made impressions on a paper drum according to sound entering a horn. The same apparatus could replay the sound from the drum.

Phonograph

In 1878 Edison began selling his phonograph (sound-writing).

Audio recording techniques were simply refined with the development of the vinyl disc, standard speeds of revolution, stereo and quadrophonic sound.

For stereo reproduction, the stylus, moving from side to side in a rotating record groove, uses the shape of the inside of the groove for the left-hand signal and that of the outside for the right. The main disadvantage is that both the record and stylus wear out.

The great breakthrough was the digital disc known as a CD in which the old revolving technologies are combined with digital coding and laser technologies to produce a cheap, easily manufactured product which is not physically affected by playing.

Early audio equipment used **valves** similar to those employed in computers.

Data storage uses audio-magnetic recording equipment from cassettes to CD technology. A cross-bred system of magnetic discs is used, both for the main hard disc in a computer and for external portable storage.

Television

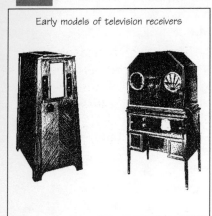

Television works by scanning across a picture for levels of brightness, a separate scan for each colour. This is much like the scanning process of reading a book.

Early models of television receivers

The brightness of the image within the camera is converted into an electrical signal which is coded and transmitted with synchronization (sync) pulses.

TV receivers extract the sync pulses and scan a screen line by line, brightening and colouring it in response to the received signal.

In 1926, John Logie Baird introduced the first usable television with a picture of 30 vertical lines, its image changing 12.5 times per second.

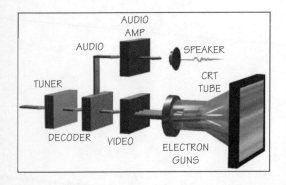

AUDIO
AMP
AUDIO
SPEAKER
TUNER
CRT
TUBE
DECODER
VIDEO
ELECTRON
GUNS

Most TVs and computer monitors use cathode ray tubes (CRTs), a sophisticated development of the thermionic valve in which applied voltages control the discharge of a stream of electrons in a vacuum.

The movie industry had settled on a standard of 24 frames per second, accommodating the physiological fact of the **persistence of vision**.

The human eye requires new information supplied to it in the form of light at least every 20th of a second for an image to seem continuous. Picture sequences presented at a slower rate seem to flicker.

A higher rate of frames gives a more 'realistic' image – reality is there all the time!

Television is broadcast as an analogue signal which must be converted to digital signals for transmission along fibre optic cable or by radio via satellites.

The universal acceptance of television both as a medium for entertainment and news and as a common cultural denominator shows how rapidly the global village has become reality.

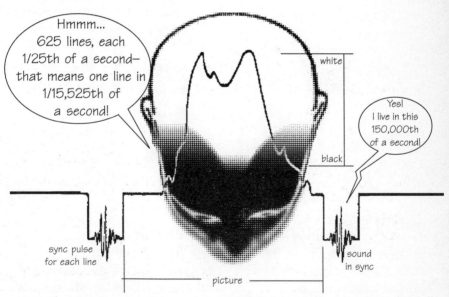

Hmmm... 625 lines, each 1/25th of a second— that means one line in 1/15,525th of a second!

white

Yes! I live in this 150,000th of a second!

black

sync pulse for each line

sound in sync

picture

Video recorders record the sync signals and each line of the image diagonally across magnetic tape. The use of a rotating drumhead in the recorder allows each image line to be about 10 cm long, much longer than the width of the tape.

Colour

 Colour is produced when light reflects off surfaces without light there is only blackness. Light is an electromagnetic wave like radio, microwaves and X-rays.

Light has different primary colours from pigments: red, blue and green. Red and green make yellow light, white needs all the colours and black no light at all.

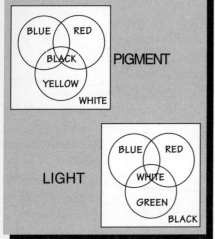

TV pictures are composed of light which is transmitted as a combination of red, green and blue (**RGB**) is the most frequent. If you look closely at your monitor screen with a magnifying glass, you can see the red, green and blue dots that make up the picture.

Looking in television shop windows, you will notice that all the pictures are a slightly different colour.

Standards of reproduction used to depend on engineers, matching a **test card** with the TV picture, but as television has proliferated, and because people are more relaxed about choosing the kind of picture they like to look at, consistent colour matters less.

In design industries, where colour matching might be crucial, the fact that the colours in a computer printout may look very different from the picture on the screen can be a matter of commercial success or failure. Artificial light also makes a difference.

Colour separations produce the complete range of colour in a picture.

Dots printed on the edges of newspapers – cyan (a bright blue), magenta (deep red), yellow and black are abbreviated to **CMYK** in printing.

Television **contrast** and **brightness** controls determine the **contrast ratio** of the image.
The human eye is capable of a huge range, a ratio of several thousands to one.
Film has a typical contrast ratio of 70:1 and TV of 30:1.

This gives an idea why film seems so much more realistic than television.

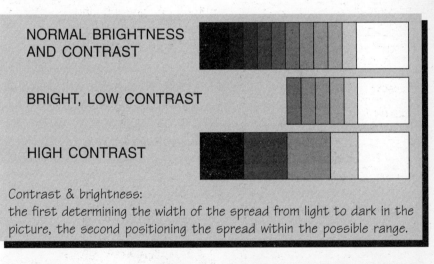

NORMAL BRIGHTNESS AND CONTRAST

BRIGHT, LOW CONTRAST

HIGH CONTRAST

Contrast & brightness:
the first determining the width of the spread from light to dark in the picture, the second positioning the spread within the possible range.

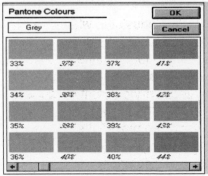

Professional colour-users have solved this problem by having an international standard set of colours of every shade and tone. These are produced by a company called **Pantone** who periodically issue new pigment cards, each with a unique identifying number, to be matched anywhere in the world.

All radio and television relies on the transmission of electromagnetic waves. Electric and magnetic fields propagate away from the source of the disturbance at the speed of light, which is the fastest speed possible.

If you turn a magnet over in your hand, its previous field which extends to infinity does not have time to collapse and the new field, now reversed locally, propagates outwards, pushing the old field away.

This slow change transmits extremely little energy, and so would be undetectable at any significant distance.

The greater the rate of this change, the more effective is the transmission.

It is easy these days to produce sufficient power at any required frequency, up to thousands of millions of cycles per second and make an aerial or antenna launch the energy into the surrounding space.

100 MHz, wavelength 3 m

200 KHz wavelength 1500 m

10 GHz, wavelength 3 cm.

Speed of light equals 299,792,458 metres per second. Wavelength of visible light lies between 4×10^{14} and $7.5 \times 10^{14.}$

Sending information requires two components – a carrier and a signal. Speech uses sound waves to carry words. Electromagnetic carriers are modulated by analogue (same shape) or digital (0s and 1s) signals by varying their amplitude (size) or frequency.

Analogue signals are applied to the carrier and vary it directly. For digital transmission, analogue information must be sampled and converted into faster binary rates of sampling, producing more accurate reproduction.

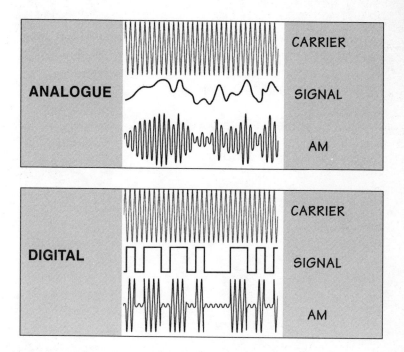

Tuning a radio you can hear 'noise' or interference.

This is evidence of the electromagnetic radiation always present throughout the universe and of signals sent on the same frequency, 'crosstalk'. This looks like snow on TV and sounds like a storm.

Digital signals are virtually immune to interference, but analogue transmission is always affected.

Transmission and display

Communication depends on transmission and presentation of information. We are familiar with a variety of technologies that send and display words and images using ...

Lasers (Light Amplification by Stimulated Emission of Radiation) which are all around us, in CD players and supermarket checkouts

Radar (RAdio Detection And Ranging)

Sonar (SOund NAvigation and Ranging)

All were used by the military, as developed from scientific research, and are now part of the satellite network.

Infrared transmission is used in remote-control carlocks and TV controllers.

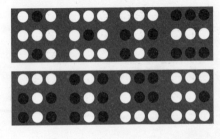

LEDs (Light Emitting Diodes) use a lot of current, so are mostly found on mains-powered equipment, e.g. clocks or moving word and picture displays.

Liquid crystal displays are cheaper, more reliable and use less current than LEDs. Found in battery-driven watches, calculators, microwaves, computers, petrol pumps and other control panels, they use the property of complex chemicals to polarize light when electrical voltage is applied. The signal supplied to the crystal determines whether or not light can pass through it. If not, it appears dark. A pattern of dark crystals can be read as a number or letter.

In a **fax** machine a light-sensitive detector converts the image into electrical signals, using an eight-tone greyscale. These tonal values are transmitted as 0s and 1s to a receiver which reconverts the signal to a paper image. An extension and refinement of **telegraphic signalling**, this technique was used in 1907 for transmitting a signal from Paris to the **Daily Mirror** in London. A minute to send a single-page document is clearly much quicker than posting it, but the quality is poor. The scan uses relatively few lines and text is treated in the same way as images, often making it illegible. To transmit text accurately requires a system of **encoding**.

signal sent

signal arriving

telephone line

The **photocopying** process was patented by Chester F. Carlson in 1938 and Xerox machines became available in 1947.

Xerography, meaning 'dry writing', works by focusing the image to be reproduced on a statically charged plate.

Dark areas retain their positive charge, attracting negatively charged powder which is then transferred to fresh paper and fixed with heat.

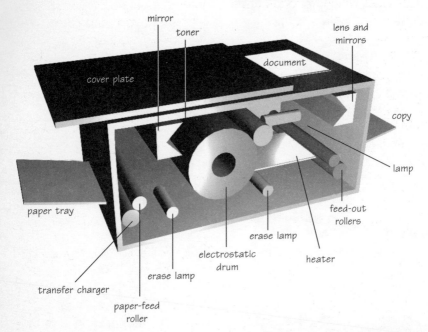

mirror
toner
lens and mirrors
document
cover plate
copy
paper tray
lamp
feed-out rollers
erase lamp
electrostatic drum
heater
transfer charger
erase lamp
paper-feed roller

The proliferation of photocopying machines made reproduction of documents easier and gave scholars access to documents too fragile to handle.

It has also come to mean that people tend not to look at the original material, saving the work of actually reading for another occasion, which may **never** arrive.

This is one of the pitfalls of hypermedia – finding and down-loading information may take precedence over actually **learning** from it.

Bar codes, found on almost all saleable products, can identify their country of origin, the producer, the sell-by date and price of the product. A check-code also makes sure the number is read correctly.

The lines are read by a **light pen** or laser which decodes the variations and sends data to a computer. In shops, this produces a till receipt and sales statistics for the retailer.

Bar codes are also used in libraries, factories and even computer games.

The global use of barcodes on products enables business to keep track of products and assists international trade.

The use of similar codes on personal identification cards will also help authorities keep track of populations and individuals. International policing authorities already have databases containing confidential information on everyone with a bank account or passport, accessible in seconds.

The control of people could be almost as simple as controlling the movements of cans of beans.

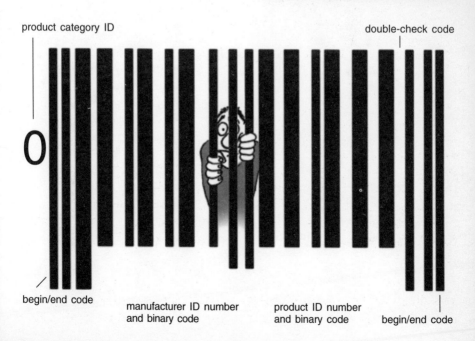

product category ID

double-check code

0

begin/end code

manufacturer ID number and binary code

product ID number and binary code

begin/end code

Through the looking glass

In 1870 John Tyndall observed that light inside a curving stream of water appeared to bend. Dr Kapany, in London in 1955, used this principle to design a light guide using strands of flexible glass. In 1966 telecom engineers realized that digital signals sent as pulses of light are immune to electrical interference.

What?

Light travelling from water into air, changes direction by a process called refraction – which is why your legs look funny in the bath!

Other advantages were that less signal would be lost, the cables would be very small, and many separate signals could be transmitted simultaneously.

The greater the range of possible signals, the larger is the **bandwidth** of the medium.

Optical fibres are capable of carrying enormous bandwidths, allowing simultaneous transmission of thousands of telephone calls, with radio and television channels operating alongside high-quality computer links.

Installation of these systems requires massive investment, but, in future, a large part of education, entertainment, work and shopping will be provided by the fibre optic networks.

Pulses of light are a perfect medium for the transmission of digital data.

Light could be directed along the lengths of glass and were first used in medicine to 'see' into the body – light was shone inside and another bundle of fibres carried the image out to a TV screen.

Bandwidth

 is the range of frequencies that can be transmitted by a particular method. Analogue bandwidth is measured in **Hertz** (cycles per second).

Multiplexing requires separate carrier frequencies, so that signals can be transmitted simultaneously without affecting each other. But several signals then need a huge bandwidth between them. The bandwidth of digital signals is measured in Bips (Bits Per Second), called baud rate.

New telephone systems are increasingly using fibre optic and other digital communications channels. A single fibre optic cable can carry many times more signals than could be transmitted over the whole available radio bandwidth.

Governments are becoming involved with the installation of high-quality communications networks. Japan and the USA have set targets in the early 21st century for the provision of nationwide networks.

'Crossed lines' mean that you can hear another person speaking on the line, a characteristic used in **phone conferencing**. An analogue telephone signal cannot send more than one signal without interference.

Normal human hearing ranges from about 30 Hz up to 15,000 Hz (or 15 kilohertz). Telephones have a bandwidth between 300 and 3 kHz.

Commercial companies are installing a worldwide communications infrastructure called ISDN (Integrated Service Digital Network) and the superior Broadband ISDN (BISDN) for providing videophone facilities, Internet connections, multichannel television and home shopping.

The ISDN network is the basis for the information superhighway, and ultimately **cyberspace**.

Modern Telephones

 Telephone exchanges have come a long way in the last twenty years. Telephone operators now frequently work from home in any part of the country, using computer terminals to supply information and control calls.

Most exchanges are automatic and capable of providing itemized bills and a range of services from call barring to last number recall.

Message services, answering machines and the mobile phone are no longer a novelty.

It is now possible to control your computer, heating and television remotely, using the telephone.

I just luv remote control!

If cyberspace were simply a matter of communication, then the telephone system is nearly there!

Broadcast media

Traditionally, broadcast media are considered to be monolithic and linear, received by a passive audience from a powerful centre.

The only truly global broadcast media are CNN, MTV and the BBC World Service. Universally recognized popstars and TV programmes, such as **Star Trek**, provide a meeting point for people who don't even speak each other's languages, an example of the global village.

Feedback to large organizations may be as efficient as participation by surfers in cyberspace. There is no guarantee that democracy will be enhanced by devolution of access to information media. Much of the information is capable of being interrogated, but not truly interactive, in that it isn't open to change.

Hundreds of TV channels do not necessarily improve quality or empower anyone.

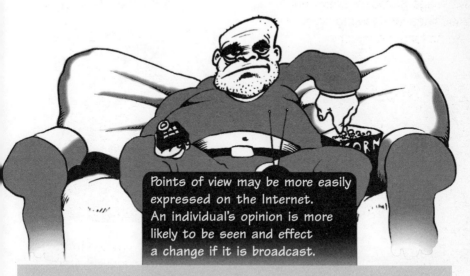

Points of view may be more easily expressed on the Internet. An individual's opinion is more likely to be seen and effect a change if it is broadcast.

The ability to express oneself to like-minded people worldwide may be an end in itself for many people, creating powerful pressure groups, but it remains to be seen if the effect is truly **enfranchising**.

Intro to computing

 We have seen that people have always sought ways of speeding things up and saving time.

We have an insatiable desire to organize, analyse and communicate what we know. The most powerful tool ever invented for doing all of these things is the computer ...

There is nothing magical about computers. They're very stupid machines that can only do what people **tell** them to do.

> Could this box really be a gate to another world?

They are almost completely without fault. If something goes wrong, probably a human did it!

What's in one?

A working store or memory, an arithmetic and logic unit (ALU), some input and output devices and a power supply.

A cooling fan is needed to blow away the heat generated by all that calculating!

Analogue machines use directly corresponding analogous quantities, such as representing changing temperature by varying the current within the 'computer', or by showing flow rates by equivalently changing voltage.

This system has the advantage of being sensitive to small changes and not requiring the transformation of physical behaviour into numbers, but is prone to errors in translation between the analogues and percentage errors introduced by inaccurate machinery in the computer which are difficult to identify or correct.

Digital computation has several advantages.

Errors are minimized by binary calculations. The procedure is abstract and is not therefore dedicated to a single physical problem as analogue machines tend to be. Digital calculations can be done at great speed, rather than in the 'real-time' of an analogue process.

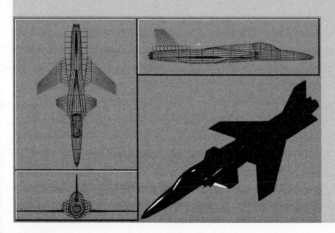

A great deal of effort is spent designing 'models' to predict analogue behaviours, using mathematical equations and algorithms (rules and procedures) that can be tested at speed, digitally.

Transcistors

The Univac (**Univ**ersal **A**utomatic **C**omputer) was the first mass-produced computer made in 1950 by the designers of ENIAC. IBM was also manufacturing machines commercially, but the days of the thermionic valve were almost over.

After all these years, we did it – a transistor!

Yeah. What do we do with it?

Invented in 1947, the transistor won its developers, John Bardeen, Walter Brattain and William Shockley of Bell Laboratories, the Nobel Prize for Physics in 1956.

The tiny and inexpensive transistor, though unreliable at first, came to perform the same functions as the thermionic valve, which was large, expensive and very fragile.

Transistors were originally made from silicon, which is defined electrically as a **semi-conductor**.
Pure silicon is electrically insulating, but **impure** silicon allows a weak current to pass through it.

For sound amplification, this current was far too small, but for making computers it was a breakthrough.

By 1957, production of transistors was up to 30 million a year.

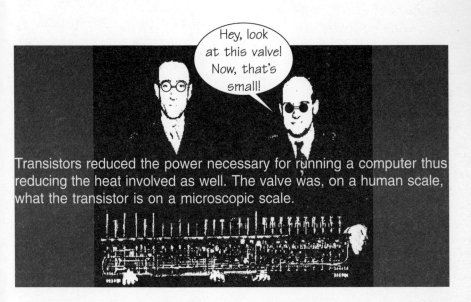

Hey, look at this valve! Now, that's small!

Transistors reduced the power necessary for running a computer thus reducing the heat involved as well. The valve was, on a human scale, what the transistor is on a microscopic scale.

Transistors were even more successful with the invention of the printed circuit board (PCB). Rather than connecting separate wires to each component, a photographic method was used to print the circuit connections as lines on a copper-coated board.
The remaining areas were then etched away with acid, leaving the lines of electrical connection behind.

Transistors and other components, such as resistors, capacitors, induction coils etc. were then soldered into place.

Remembering 0 and 1

Ideal for use in the electronic components of the modern computer, the transistors can be switched ON or OFF, representing 1 or 0 in the logic sequence. Each number, 1 or 0, is a binary digit or **bit** (Binary digiT), and is the basic unit of information in a digital computer.

Several bits together are called a **word** and a standard word length of 8 bits (256 different possible combinations) is called a **byte**. Computers can now handle longer words of 16, 32 or even 64 bits.

At the heart of the computer is the CPU or Central Processing Unit. The CPU handles numbers and adds or subtracts them according to binary instructions. The CPU takes numbers from the computer memory and sends them back when they have been processed.

Memory in a computer is rather different from human memory. We forget things easily, rarely remember trivial details, and allow our emotions to affect our memories.

Computer memory is more like a storage room or set of pigeon-holes, each with its own label or address.

Every binary number that the computer deals with is sent to a particular pigeon-hole which in turn has an address code, another binary number. In this way, each piece of information can be reliably identified, retrieved, processed and returned to memory without loss or error.

A CPU with a 10-bit address code can locate 1024 addresses, usually called 'one kilobyte' of memory. Kilo is the standard unit prefix meaning one thousand in base ten, so one would expect 1 kilobyte, to be 1000 bytes.

Since there is no simple conversion at these values between base 2 and base 10, the computer world has taken liberties with the vocabulary – when it says 1kb it means 1024 bytes, an internationally accepted meaning.

A 20-bit memory is really 1,048,576 bytes, rounded down in computer language to one megabyte (1Mb).

Current personal computers normally have between 2Mb and 16Mb of RAM fitted.

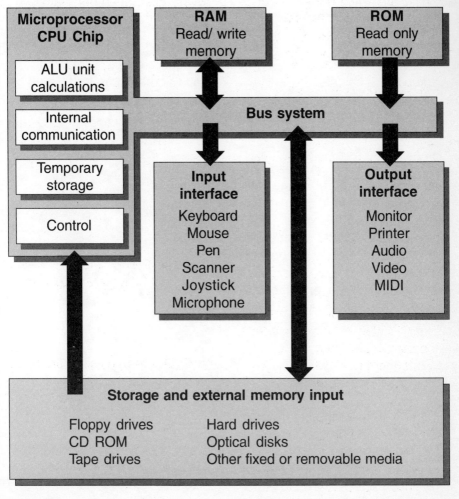

Microprocessor CPU Chip

- ALU unit calculations
- Internal communication
- Temporary storage
- Control

RAM
Read/ write memory

ROM
Read only memory

Bus system

Input interface
Keyboard
Mouse
Pen
Scanner
Joystick
Microphone

Output interface
Monitor
Printer
Audio
Video
MIDI

Storage and external memory input

Floppy drives
CD ROM
Tape drives

Hard drives
Optical disks
Other fixed or removable media

What's RAM? Just keep reading...

Well, first, the internal memory of the computer is divided into two parts, one which holds information that the computer cannot change, called Read-Only Memory.

The Basic Input/Output System (BIOS) information, built into computers to perform the initial start up and test hardware functions, remains in ROM, whether or not the computer is powered. Portable and laptop machines also hold software in ROM.

The other type of memory is Random-Access Memory or RAM. The CPU can reach any address in RAM in any order – it is the workshop where the computer does its processing. RAM normally retains information when power is supplied to the computer, but anything that you were working on in RAM will disappear when the computer is switched off.

Permanently required information must be 'saved'. Most computers have at least one internal disc drive called a 'hard drive', a permanent storage facility on which data is recorded.

The magnetic material is disc-shaped and rotates under a magnetic recording head. A blank disc is divided into addressed segments by a procedure called 'formatting'. Each address can be located and its contents changed.

Not very hard these discs, are they?

The processing power of a computer is determined by the speed and amount of RAM fitted and the speed of the CPU.

Computers in domestic use in the 1990s have more processing power than the one that first put men on the Moon.

ASCII

All digital computers can actually do is add, subtract and compare binary numbers. Everything else we want them to do must involve combinations and repetitions of those functions.

At the simplest level, to multiply 476,533,212.678 by 976, a computer goes through a procedure of adding 476,533,212.678 to itself 976 times. The greater the power of the computer, the more quickly it can do this.

When dealing with numbers and letters input, the computer has to convert them from denary base 10 to binary base 2.

Letters and symbols are coded as 0s and 1s according to an internationally agreed system called ASCII (pronounced 'askey') table – the American Standard Code for Information Interchange. Each letter or symbol on a standard Western keyboard is assigned an 8-digit code, so that the computer can convert keyboard instructions into numbers it can then manipulate and store.

Extra letters can be generated for the large numbers of characters in Eastern languages by using the normal keys in combination with other command keys on the keyboard: shift, control, alternative, option.
Several hundred codes can be generated by the operator of an ordinary keyboard.

part of ASCII table

A	1000001	N	1001110
B	1000010	O	1001111
C	1000011	P	1010000
D	1000100	Q	1010001
E	1000101	R	1010010
F	1000110	S	1010011
G	1000111	T	1010100
H	1001000	U	1010101
I	1001001	V	1010110
J	1001010	W	1010111
K	1001011	X	1011000
L	1001100	Y	1011001
M	1001101	Z	1011010

What does this say?

1010111 1100101 1101100 1100011
1101111 1101101 1100101 0100000
1110100 1101111 0100000 1100011
1111001 1100010 1100101 1110010
1110011 1110000 1100001 1100011
1100101 0100001

Telling computers what to do

 Computers are simple creations that respond to very simple commands.

Most understand less than 200 instructions, each presented to the computer as an 8-bit numeric code which the computer interprets to carry out functions.

SUB!

MOV!

I don't speak computer **mnemonic**, sorry!

Programmes in **machine code** are simple, very slow to write but fast and efficient.

The simplest language is **assembly** with pretty much a 1 to 1 relationship between programme instructions and code.

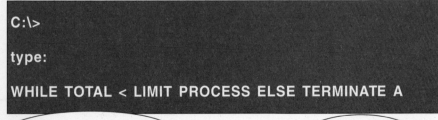

```
C:\>

type:

WHILE TOTAL < LIMIT PROCESS ELSE TERMINATE A
```

I don't understand that!

neither do I...

But stupid computers do!

Higher-level languages are much more intelligible to people but still far from what a machine can understand ...

* a++
** MALLOC

* a+1
** Memory allocation

Those high-level instructions are translated into machine code by a programme called **compiler**.

Compiling usually takes some time, but the programmes run much faster.

There are languages, called **interpreters** that do not need compiling, since their instructions are interpreted by the system at the time of execution. One such language is **'Smalltalk'**.

I DON'T NEED ANY COMPILERS!

Systems analysis

Systems analysis is almost completely associated with computers, but unless analysts can assess a situation comprehensively and accurately, they cannot make it computable. Diagrams are a good way to start. For example – how do you make a cup of tea?

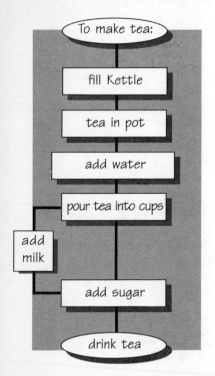

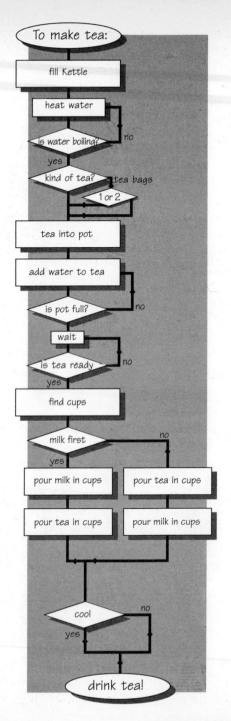

A first sequence produces many possible additional instructions, questions and options.

Flow diagrams such as this are a very useful way of translating real-life problems into the kind of activity a computer can be made to do, in this case an automated drinks machine.

My mummy is very intelligent, you know... She's had to do lots of analysis before my birth!

A refinement of the simple YES/NO option is provided by expert systems in which it is possible to allocate probabilities to certain options, so that the outcome can be given a percentage reliability.

Ya, ya, according to my calculations, you should have an embrella right now in zis room!

For example, asking an expert weather prediction system about the need for an umbrella on a particular day could involve temperature and barometer readings fed into the database of the machine, together with probabilities derived from previous weather patterns.

In Britain, where the weather is uncertain, it would no doubt tell you to take one just in case!

A learning system would continually update its information and generate rules and probabilities from its own database, indicating the beginnings of an **artificial intelligence**.

Cyberspace time – will it free us?

 Traditional clocks are analogue displays, because they show time passing. Modern digital display shows only numbers pertaining to the moment.

The superiority of the iconographic analogue display becomes increasingly important as people use computers.

Only computer buffs are particularly interested in what the computer is doing and how it is doing it. For the rest of us, being able to operate the machine is more important.

The aspect of computer use which makes the most difference to the user is the **interface** – where the user and the machine meet.

The most effective communications display uses graphics and symbols or 'icons'. This is usually referred to by the abbreviation GUI standing for Graphical User Interface. Macintosh and MS Windows have similar visual displays using a system of menus.

Counting the vibrations of atoms uses smaller lengths of time, enabling greater accuracy than counting crystal vibrations. The natural vibrations of atoms of **caesium**, 9,192,631,770 times a second, replaced the old measure of a unit of time, based on the Earth's rotation as the international standard **caesium** in 1967.

Clocks counting the vibrations of the **ammonia** atom, 23,870,129,300 per second, are accurate to 1 second in 1,700,000 years and are used in navigation systems for high–speed aircraft and missiles.

Each clock pulse advances all the operations of the computer by one step. Everything is synchronous.

In some programmes, an animated watch icon appears when the computer is busy doing something... to show you that it is actually doing something.

Powerful communications devices using high-speed computers have given birth to cyberspace. At nearly 24 million oscillations each second, they can perform millions of calculations per second.

The rhythm of life has radically changed. The arbitrary division of time into hours, minutes and seconds made people feel like automata, under the control of the machines they were employed to operate.

The speed of computer clocks is too fast to feel on a human scale, but serves to reinforce the power of **Standard Time**. An optimistic interpretation of the move towards teleworking or telematics (computerized connection into the home for the dual purposes of work and leisure, *direct contact with cyberspace*), is to imagine the high-tech home as an isolated country idyll, allowing its inhabitants to rediscover nature and the times of the seasons. Maybe.

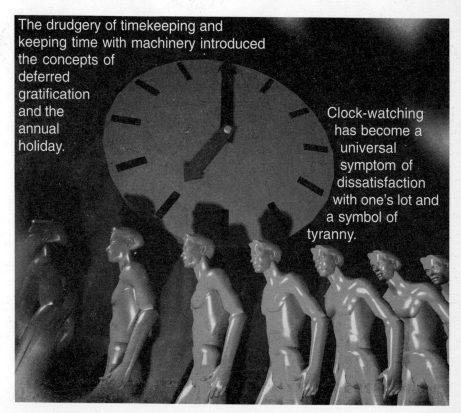

The drudgery of timekeeping and keeping time with machinery introduced the concepts of deferred gratification and the annual holiday.

Clock-watching has become a universal symptom of dissatisfaction with one's lot and a symbol of tyranny.

Booting up

To understand cyberspace, in which millions of computers worldwide are connected together, it's important to know about the equipment you are using.

The term 'computer' in normal conversation tends to mean *all* the equipment used and a particular programme. Still, it's all relative...

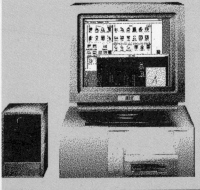

INPUTS

The greatest volume of data input to hardware comes from other hardware.

A computer usually consists of a visual display unit and a box containing the processor, memory, floppy disk and other storage drives, a power supply and all the interface circuitry required to get them to work together and to interface with those outside.

The latter are the keyboard, screen, other storage and output devices and perhaps a communication link.
When switched on, it goes through a start-up routine called **booting up.**

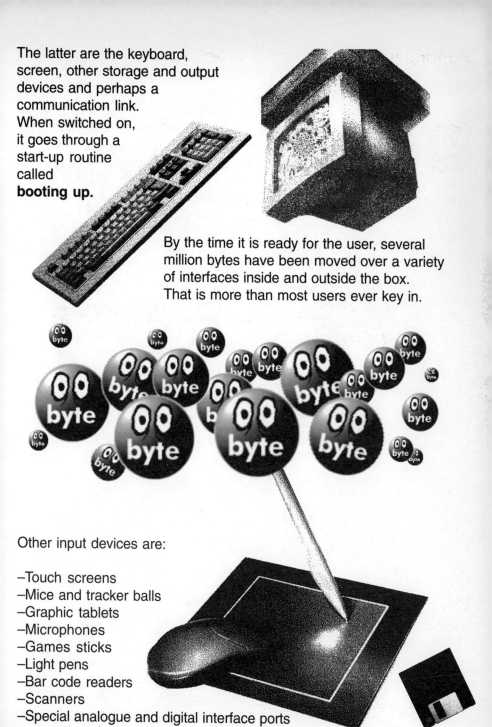

By the time it is ready for the user, several million bytes have been moved over a variety of interfaces inside and outside the box. That is more than most users ever key in.

Other input devices are:

–Touch screens
–Mice and tracker balls
–Graphic tablets
–Microphones
–Games sticks
–Light pens
–Bar code readers
–Scanners
–Special analogue and digital interface ports

Let me output ...

All data coming out of an item of computer hardware is an output – the whole point of running the computer is to produce useful outputs.

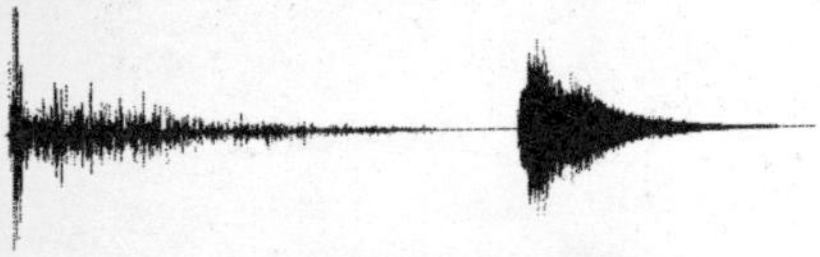

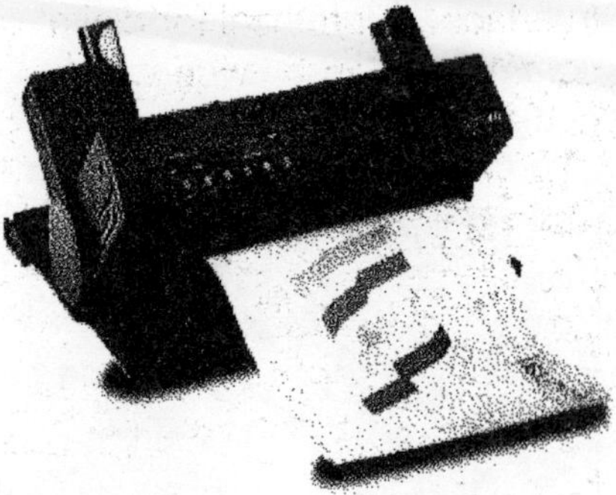

These may be screen displays, printed hard copy, sound, Braille, digital and analogue signals, which may be applied to control equipments and data for transmission to other machines.

Output devices:

printers–
black and white or colour
daisy-wheel, dot-matrix,
laser, bubble-jet, plotters

modems–
(MOdulator/ DEModulator) to transmit signals along telephone or other cables

loudspeakers.

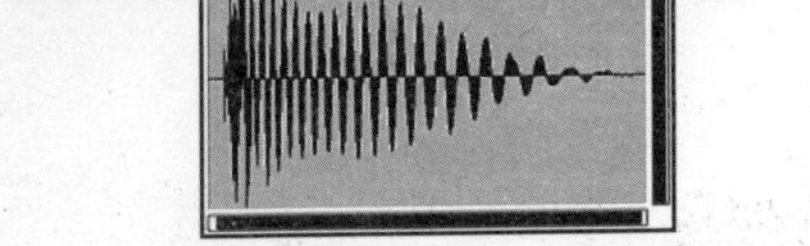

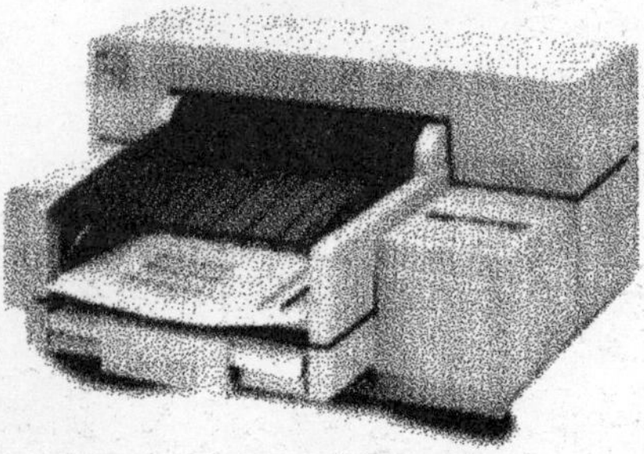

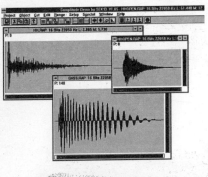

The output is not necessarily text – it can be music notation, electrical control signals to machinery, synthetic voice equipment ...

The connection between personal computers and music began with the introduction of **MIDI** (Musical Instrument Digital Interface), a protocol for digital communication between electronic instruments.

The first personal computer with a built-in MIDI interface was Atari ST, which quickly became a platform of choice for many musicians.

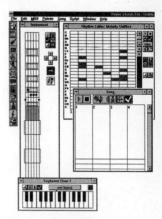

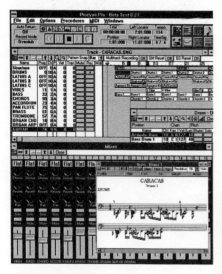

The emerging multimedia technologies and hard disc recording (digital recording of audio material straight to a computer's hard disc) are opening previously undreamed-of possibilities for artistic expression and new forms for musicians and composers.

Face to face

As you read this, you are one side of an **interface**.
The other side is text printed on a sheet of paper.
This is a one-way interface powered by ambient lighting.

Equipment making up a computer system has interfaces for each connection, comprising a physical link and a set of rules defining what can be passed, how it is passed and the way the passing will be controlled.

Both sides of an interface must be set up to an agreed standard or it will not work.

One piece of equipment sends a signal to another to indicate that it has data to send.

The receiving equipment prepares itself, then replies 'OK transmit'. The first then sends the data and a check code to counteract error. When an error is detected, a re-transmission request is issued.

This clever system of error detection makes enormous data exchange systems like the Internet possible.

The most easily recognized interface for personal computer use is the screen, usually a CRT (Cathode Ray Tube, as in a television). This is NOT the computer! It's an output device showing what is happening in the computer, which usually lives in a separate box.

It is common to operate computers with text-based interfaces without a real-time output on a screen, e.g. MS-DOS or your bank cashpoint or ATM 'Automatic Telling Machine'.

Tell me!
TELL ME!
Did I do good?
Was I OK?
Did they like me?

A recent breakthrough for blind computer users has been the invention of a mouse with a Braille interface using memory-metal rods which 'read' text on screen as the cursor passes over it.

Previously, Braille texts had to be printed out or read with a text scanner which had to scroll the whole document in sequence. The new mouse produces Braille symbols under the fingertip of the user, giving freedom to scan quickly and randomly across the screen.

We humans like to see what we're doing, and it makes errors apparent if our instructions are visible on screen. We need **feedback**.

Data storage

 Working with data requires a very rapid access to its storage.

Currently used programmes need to be accessed with every instruction and backing store of programme and data files, require frequent access.

Back-up storage of programmes and data files, need retrieval in case of computer failure, while archive storage is used for historical data.

The punched card system of data storage was still in use in commercial computing in the UK into the 1970s, then came punched paper tape, uncannily similar to Turing's data model for his analytical engine.
Surfaces coated with magnetic material could record data as variable magnetic field. These came in the form of cards, drums, tape and discs which moved relative to separate or combined read/write heads. Discrete valves and transistors had also been used before the development of the memory chip.

In the early days of computing, the most adaptable and versatile magnetic storage system available was the domestic audio-cassette tape. But then, revolving discs using a magnetic surface similar to that of the tape made access to the data quicker and easier and became the most popular option.

Adaptable and reliable methods of holding, copying and transmitting data both within and between computers have since been designed. Transportable copies are small and secure, the most common being floppy discs.

Floppy disc is a convenient means of storage and transfer, but access and transfer are much slower than for hard discs.

Hard drives feature metal discs built into their casing, sometimes in stacks.
Standard 3.5 inch floppy discs normally hold up to 2 megabytes of data. Other portable media include minidiscs and CDs which hold vast data quantities.

Magnetic tape using short standard cassettes in ordinary players (and thereby involving a high proportion of error) is still used for back-up.
Digital Audio Tape (DAT) mini-discs and laser discs (which can digitally record and playback) have excellent quality that doesn't diminish with use in the way that audio tapes do.

The equivalent recording facility for CD-ROMs will enable wider distribution of home-produced archives and entertainment to supplement the encyclopedias and reference works commercially available.
CD-ROM (Compact Disc ROM) uses the same technology as music CDs – digital data in the form of dots on a reflective surface containing programmes and data instead of music. Other optical storage such as WORM (Write Once Read Many) devices are available.

Hard disc storage capacities range from under 100 Mbytes to thousands of Mbytes, with access time of a few milliseconds.

Over the last 25 years, the size, reliability, performance and price of storage, as with processing units, have improved 100 to 1000 times.

LIMERICK COUNTY LIBRARY

O/Sweet machines!

 Operating systems (O/S) interpret keyboard commands, send data to the screen, read and write disk files and utility tasks, e.g. time-keeping. Just about all computer use involves these actions. So, rather than every programme duplicating them, a standard set of instructions is applied while operating the system, interfacing between the software and machine code.

Early computers had their own operating systems which couldn't be used on other machines.

The first generally applicable O/S was called CP/M, originally 'Control Printer/Monitor' although it has now come to mean 'Control Program for Microcomputers'. Applications based on CP/M could be run on many different machines.

The most widely used O/S is **MS-DOS** (MicroSoft Disc Operating System) produced by Microsoft, headed by Bill Gates, one of the world's richest men. He realized early on that greater profits were to be made from software than from hardware. MS-DOS is designed for use on personal computers compatible with IBM PCs.

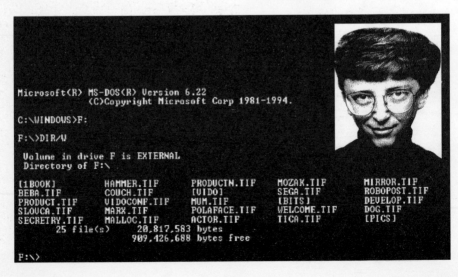

There is often a little confusion here – a **personal computer** is any small self-contained system.

The one made by IBM became the industry standard, cleverly named the PC! Most other manufacturers have endorsed the standard, so that many machines, as well as being pcs (personal computers) are also PC compatible.
An Amiga, Macintosh or Atari is also a pc, though not a PC!

A more complex and professional O/S is UNIX which is common on multi-user machines, especially in academic and commercial situations. Much of the Internet is based on UNIX.
MS-DOS and other text-based systems commercially available, involve the user in learning the equivalent of a new language in order to give instructions to the computer.

Look, I'm tellin' you – this is DOS! If it says C:\> and floppy is labeled A:, it must be DOS!

Oh yeah? And how do you know? You've only ever used a Mac!

The MS-DOS commands are relatively simple but have to be typed in accurately with the correct 'grammar' and in the right order.
This is OK for people who work with computers all the time but very irritating for the rest of us who just want to use the computer to make life easier.

First **Graphical User Interface** (GUI), was pioneered by Rank Xerox.

A breakthrough in domestic computing was the development of the **Macintosh** operating system by Wozniak and Jobs who started Apple computers in 1976. They designed the GUI that was more appealing and easier to use than text instructions in DOS.

The most widely used GUI, known as **MS Windows** is produced by Microsoft.

Small pictures (icons) representing applications, folders, files, or the wastebasket appear on screen and they can all be dragged into required position using the mouse.

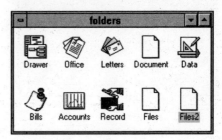

Rather than typing in instructions, the user simply has to select between those on offer, hardly ever using the keyboard.

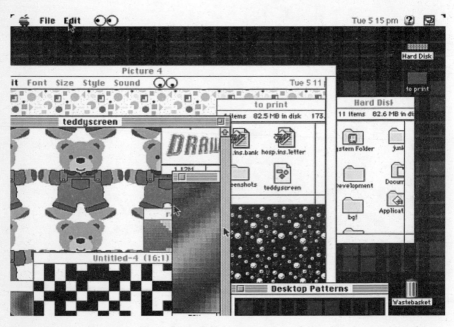

The disadvantage is that GUI O/S uses a lot of the basic processing power of the computer.

Even a nervous newcomer to computers will be able to use any GUI in minutes, since all the instructions are in (American) English (or other standard languages), and most of the options only require you to point an arrow and click a button.

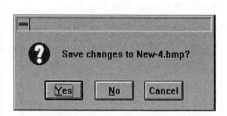

If you do something 'wrong', the machine will double-check with you.

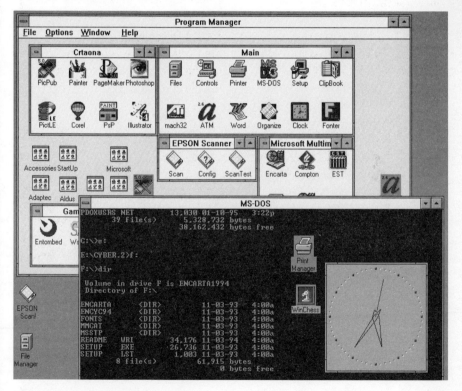

The dream of all users is the absolute compatibility of a 'cross-platform' which would allow any O/S to be used on all machines.

Yeah, that's Cyberspace!!!

Languages

 Instructions can be devised to make a computer do anything in the way of processing data. It will blindly and faithfully follow the instructions, working through the program and data until a stop condition is reached, an error condition occurs or the power is switched off.

What a particular machine can do is dependent purely on the wit and care of the writer of the instruction list, the **programmer**. A good programmer requires a thorough knowledge of the language being used, but even more important is the ability to analyse problems, recognize patterns and concepts, and to think clearly.

Computers only understand machine code, which is the lowest level of computer language.

Ordinary users have great difficulty with this because it is numeric code, translated into binary, denoting specific operations. People can explain their requirements more quickly and with less errors in our natural language than in numeric codes.

Languages have been defined specially for different computer uses – engineering, data-processing etc. – and can usually be made to work on many different kinds of computer, using the appropriate compiler.

Grace Hopper, now over 90

The first computer languages, known as **von Neumann languages**, emerged from programmes that were written in the 1950s to write machine code more efficiently.

FORTRAN (FORmula TRANslation language), very popular and still common today. Most appropriate for scientific calculations and not easy to use for commercial applications.

In the 1950s, Grace Hopper produced a language that would understand English – COBOL (COmmon Business Oriented Language).

A standard procedure for scripting mathematical formulae called Algol (ALGOrithmic Language) was introduced into FORTRAN, allowing improvements in programming.

BASIC (Beginners' All-purpose Symbolic Instruction Code), most popular of the early languages, in use worldwide within a very short time. The user can 'run' small sections of the programme to check them.

Combining BASIC and Algol produced Pascal, similar to a very popular language used throughout the personal and commercial computing arena: C and its variations C++ and Turbo C.

In the early 1980s, the US Defense Department developed a military language – ADA (after Babbage's collaborator Ada King). A crucial part of the Star Wars programme, it was designed for 'reacting to world events as they happen' ... fingers on the button!

All these languages start with machine code and build up to words and symbols that become familiar with use.
An alternative approach is to begin with ordinary language statements or questions and break them down into their essential parts to arrive at simple words which can be translated to machine code.

The first of these LISt Processing languages, LISP, is common in research areas such as artificial intelligence.

There is a price to pay for the benefits of high-level languages. They are less flexible, can be difficult for some problems, and are not as efficient as well-written low-level code.

Just as the GUI has made computing accessible to a wider range of people, new ways of programming using ordinary language instructions are becoming available and are especially important as voice-controlled machinery makes its appearance.

Soft (but not squidgy) ware

Software includes all programmes, applications and operating systems, all the coding and organizing information needed to make computers perform tasks – controlling a washing-machine, a programming language, a word processor or an operating system.
Software is held as one or more files, just as data is.

Software for computing activities, such as programming, enables people to learn to be programmers and write more software. It is possible to buy different operating systems and programming languages, just as you can shop for other software such as games.
Applications software is so named because the computer's capabilities are applied to make ordinary activities easier or quicker.

Typing becomes word-processing.
Accounting uses automatically calculated spreadsheets.
Technical drawing becomes a flexible tool for designers.

Software engineering involves analysing a requirement, design and production of programmes and systems to meet it, together with the specification of hardware requirements, implementation of the resulting system and its subsequent maintenance.

OK, OK...
We'll continue software testing as soon as they finish the game!

A range of programmes have been devised for use by software engineers including tools for analysis and software preparation, testing and de-bugging and documentation.

A **bug** is a problem in the logic sequence of the programme which makes it do the wrong thing. The bug is often only a grammatical error, equivalent to a spelling mistake or a missed full stop, but it can cause enormous damage or crash the programme.

Applications software covers everything from games to nuclear power stations and defence systems. The range of complexity is enormous, as is the range of consequences of programme errors.
Rigorous proof of correctness and testing is therefore needed.

Well, it seems you've got some bugs in the system, but not to worry, an expert is checking it right now!

The word 'bug' comes from the time when computers were built using valves which glowed, attracting insects. The bugs would get into the machinery and cause electrical faults within the computer.

Modern operating systems and applications packages are very complex, but for normal use on personal computers the consequences of error are not too serious.

It seems common practice to issue new software to selected users (beta test sites) for a short trial period before selling to the general public.

Much applications software provides for the user to make limited adjustments to the way it operates.

Users can tailor databases, spreadsheets and few other applications to meet their own particular needs, but for more complicated requirements, an appropriate programming language is needed.

Databases and spreadsheets

 Databases and spreadsheets are two of the most widely used packages available.

Database packages contain files or tables in which data can be stored like an electronic card file. Each 'card' is a record containing several fields.

For example, a database might be generated by a computer retailer, so that advertising could be mailed to likely customers.
A relational database consists of several related tables with a couple of fields in common,so that more specific markets can be aimed at.

A spreadsheet is an electronic representation of a large sheet of paper divided by rules into rows and columns of cells.

The computer screen acts as a window which can be moved over the sheet allowing any part to be seen.

Each cell can contain text, a number or a formula and is referred to by a column/row address. A wide range of mathematical, logical and reference functions are usually provided and data can be transferred to and from databases and word processors.

Word processing and desktop publishing

 Ease of correction when using a computer instead of a typewriter has made the computer a cheap, effective and versatile tool for producing finished documents. Now almost anyone can produce a perfect document using a spell checker, syntax and style checkers.

The ability of word processors to customize standard letters and edit text also reduces the amount of keying required. This has led to a great increase in productivity.

The quality of output of some quite cheap printers is such that anyone with a personal computer can publish their own books.

The printing revolution around 1500 introduced standard typefaces, called fonts, and text sizes which are still in use today.

For home typewriting, the characteristic Courier typewriter font gives equal width space to each letter, like this ...

Quick brown fox jumps over the lazy dog

Modern fonts arrange letters proportionate to their sizes ...

Times:
Quick brown fox jumps over the ...

Impact:
Quick brown fox jumps over the ...

Most word processing programmes offer a range of fonts in various sizes, measured in points or picas:

9 point   *9 italic*
12 point   **12 bold**
18 point

36 point

Professional quality typography and layout, with spreadsheets, pictures, mailing lists etc., allows desktop publishing (dtp) to manipulate both text and pictures over multiple page documents.

Many printing companies now accept computer discs instead of pasted-up pages, with printing plates being made by computer-controlled equipment directly from the disc.
The whole of this very book was produced on a computer!

In the 1970s and 1980s, this worldwide revolution in typography and typesetting profoundly affected the printing industry, especially in newspaper production.
Most journalists now type their stories directly into a computer, where it is edited and positioned by other journalists.

Old specialist trades, such as typesetting and layout design, have declined as workers carry out a greater range of tasks.
The skills of typography and design are still as valuable however, and possibly even more sought after.

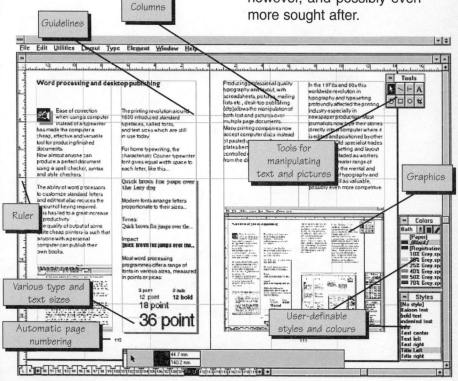

QWERTY, the standard English language keyboard layout, designed by Sholes, has been in use since 1890s.
Just as A4 paper has become standard, and machinery built to deal with that size, QWERTY keyboards are universal and unlikely to change until voice recognition technologies are well advanced and cheap.

Repetitive Strain Injury (RSI), resulting from hundreds of small movements of the wrist and fingers, causes severe pain and incapacity.

Traditional typewriters need force and movement, but computer keyboards and mouse buttons only require small tense actions. Happily, electronic keyboards don't suffer from the typewriter problem of jammed keys.

Although RSI affects an increasing number of people, it is not yet accepted as a serious medical disorder.

The major effect of wordprocessing has been to reduce the level of skills needed for secretarial work.

The next major step will be to remove the secretary entirely, replacing her with voice recognition technology and smart software that can do all the work of preparing documents, organizing meetings and making coffee!

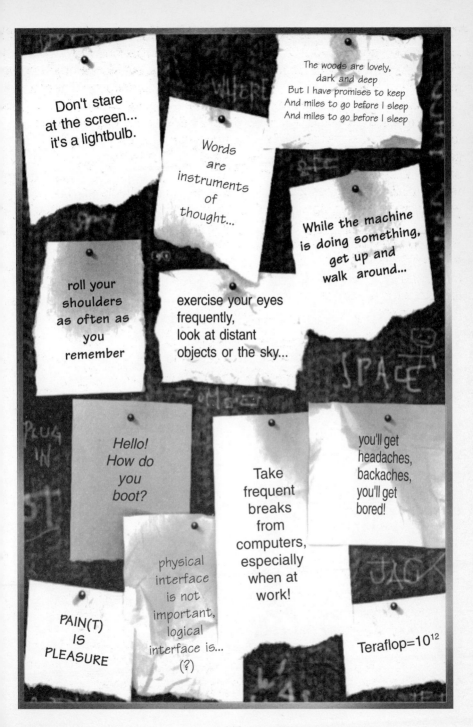

Don't stare at the screen... it's a lightbulb.

The woods are lovely, dark and deep
But I have promises to keep
And miles to go before I sleep
And miles to go before I sleep

Words
are
instruments
of
thought...

While the machine is doing something, get up and walk around...

roll your shoulders as often as you remember

exercise your eyes frequently, look at distant objects or the sky...

Hello!
How do
you
boot?

Take frequent breaks from computers, especially when at work!

you'll get headaches, backaches, you'll get bored!

physical interface is not important, logical interface is...
(?)

PAIN(T)
IS
PLEASURE

Teraflop=10^{12}

Paint and draw

Painting applications use very similar principles: mark-making 'instruments', such as pencils, brushes and spray cans in various shapes and sizes, and drawing tools to create, select or isolate chosen shapes.

Analogous to drawing equipment in the real world, these are operated using a mouse or pen interface.

Most painting programmes use a system known as bit-mapping, similar to weaving in its use of coordinates to determine the location of particular coloured squares or pixels (picture or pix elements).

The position of each bit is recognized by the computer, and a colour is mapped as required. Every new instruction changes the colour of each square.

Screen shot of a basic paint programme with limited capabilities.

The type and size of the computer video memory determines the range of available colours: B&W, greyscale, 256 or millions.

If you draw a circle one pixel thick:

most bit-map programmes will neither know or remember that there was a circle.

This allows you to erase or change it.

Advanced paint software simulates any natural medium and even allows the user to create custom tools, canvases and multiple light sources.

An alternative drawing paradigm uses object-oriented methods. In this system, when you draw a circle, the computer remembers the mathematical formulae required to reproduce the shape.

Object can be moved, rotated, reflected and distorted, copied or pasted and its colour, size, shape or proportions can be changed.

It is possible to take away certain parts of an object or to 'weld' other shapes on it. It is like collage, with the extra facility of changing the attributes of the pieces at any given session.

■ + ● = 🔑 - □ = ⌐

Whereas bit-mapped images are equivalent to painting, object-oriented methods are more like sculpture, filling flexible wire frames with colours and textures, copying them and building up layers.

Object-oriented drawing programme

A bit-mapped image file has to contain information about every point, even on the unpainted portions and these files can be huge. Object-oriented drawings are usually much smaller for storage.

before
and now...

Bit-mapped text used to look jagged because it is made up of squares, but modern software uses anti-aliasing to minimize this.

Object-oriented page description languages, such as PostScript, treat each letter as an object, calculating the curves and lines needed to draw it pecisely.

cyberspace cyberspace cyberspace cyberspace cyberspace cyberspace cyberspace cyberspace

Many drawing software packages are incredibly easy to use, enabling beginners to concentrate on design rather than labour over technical drawing skills.

Computer Aided Design uses OOP (Object-Oriented Programmes) to make representations of both 2D and 3D machinery or structures. These can then be tested under simulated stresses within the computer.

Rapid prototyping uses CAD designs to produce 3D print-outs, laser-hardened plastic models of 3D objects, useful for product design and ergonomic testing before production.

It is possible to design things within the cyberspace of the computer that are impossible to build. Rather than bringing those objects into the real world, we can go into **virtual reality** to experiment with them!

Finished designs can be sent directly from the CAD system to computer-controlled machinery which can cut or drill materials to exact specifications. CNC (Computer Numerical Controlled) machines enable CAM (Computer Aided Manufacturing). CAD/CAM is a common subject of study in engineering courses and a useful skill in most design areas.

3D visualization programs are not usually as exact as CAD because their purpose is to represent the world or a fantasy environment to the eyes, not provide construction blueprints.

In 3D 'worlds' every object and surface must be constructed and rendered with colour and texture.

Most programmes use solids to represent shapes or polygons, where a surface approximates to a plane. The smaller the shapes it uses, the more real the image will look.

Reality is seen as infinitely small dots of colour.

To draw a triangle at a particular point in a picture, the computer has to plot a starting point, calculate the directions and lengths of the lines, and for 3D possibilities, hold in its memory any information about what happens in the direction we can't see.

Movement in 3D world isn't merely three dimensional. Both sensors and input devices have 6 degrees of freedom, as well as the three standard Cartesian directions (xyz) movements called **roll**, **pitch** and **yaw,** are also controllable.

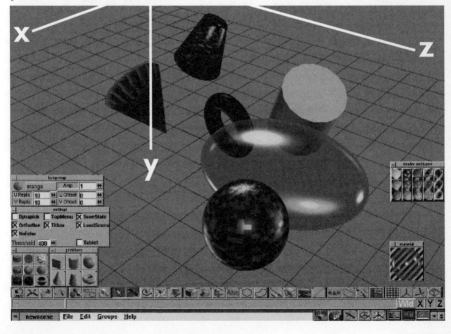

For every picture, the computer performs hundreds or thousands of these calculations, depending on the desired resolution of the image, the shape and position of the polygons.

The process of assigning the correct colour, light levels and reflections to make each shape in the scene look realistic, requires even more calculations.

If the image is still, these calculations can be given time.

Even animations are planned and linear and can be prepared over time before being assembled.
Interactive 3D worlds, such as virtual reality (VR), allow the viewer to choose where to look and travel, so the computer must have an incredibly fast processor.

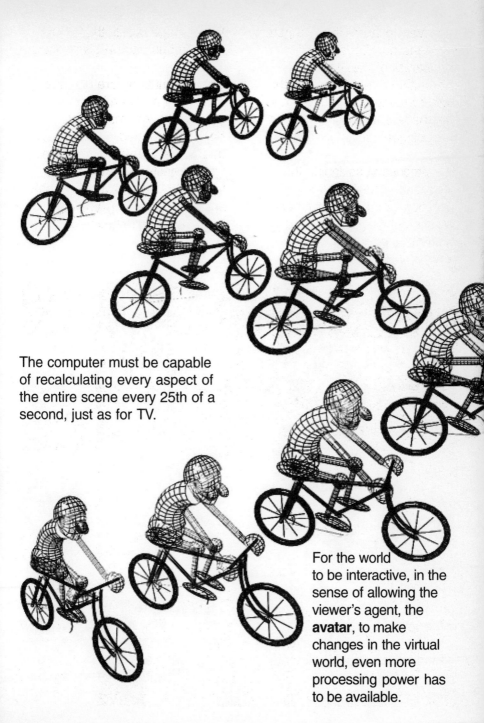

The computer must be capable of recalculating every aspect of the entire scene every 25th of a second, just as for TV.

For the world to be interactive, in the sense of allowing the viewer's agent, the **avatar**, to make changes in the virtual world, even more processing power has to be available.

Virtually real

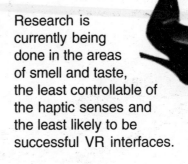

 This is an ideal interface with cyberspace, total immersion in the virtual world, using a headset giving stereoscopic visual and audio inputs, a tactile body suit and data gloves for experience and control of the environment, and machinery to change gravity so that you can float or fly!

Research is currently being done in the areas of smell and taste, the least controllable of the haptic senses and the least likely to be successful VR interfaces.

Touch is equally difficult to reproduce artificially, especially if it involves sensations that bruise or scratch!

Its more likely to feel one's skin creep while reading a book than to produce a body suit capable of conveying every touch from the lightest tickle to a vigourous rub, from a sensuous embrace to a sound thrashing.

Because sight is the predominant sense, we suspend our disbelief if convincing visual information is presented to us. Introduction of appropriate sound, touch and movement can lead to entirely believable virtual worlds.

Human desires for immersion in other worlds and for bodies in different shapes and sizes have been apparent in religion, ritual and dance for thousands of years.

Recreation and pleasure are major driving forces in the development of virtual interactivity.

An Internet sex doll called Virtual Valerie is proving very popular.

It is possible both on the Internet in text-based MUDs and in future VR worlds to present yourself as a fantasy creature, acting out fantasies and dreams.

The dream of another body will increase the perception of the self as an object, since internal experience will inevitably be of the real body.

You'll still want to eat and drink. You'll still get tired.

CYBER SEX

119

The science fiction alternative to this has been eloquently described by Pat Cadigan whose characters sell their memories to VR dealers, jacking in directly to the brain and bypassing the senses.

A similar scenario occurs in the Schwarzenegger film **Total Recall**, in which the hero cannot tell if he has really travelled to the Moon or not.

Does it matter?

Towards the end of the 20th century, work is becoming scarce in the rich countries and areas of unspoilt natural beauty are protected and designated world parks.
It seems likely that work and travel will become a privilege for the rich, and that most people will have to resort to pleasure-seeking in virtual reality.

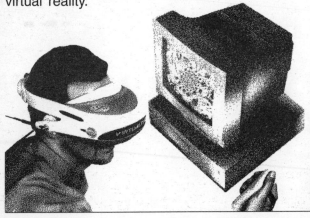

VR simulators to date have been used to train pilots and doctors, but research is mostly driven and financed by the entertainment and military industries.

The major drawback with VR so far is that of virtual motion sickness, when the body experiences real gravitational forces even more effective than those produced by a roller coaster!

Until completely 'natural' virtual experience is possible with faster computers and more responsive software, the VR user is neither fully in the virtual world, like the avatar, nor completely aware of the real world.

Other serious uses of VR are in the areas of physics, chemistry and genetics where manipulation of real molecules using virtual objects creates new materials.

Bizarre physical laws can be introduced, such as occur in space or at molecular levels, to produce more effective models of reality.

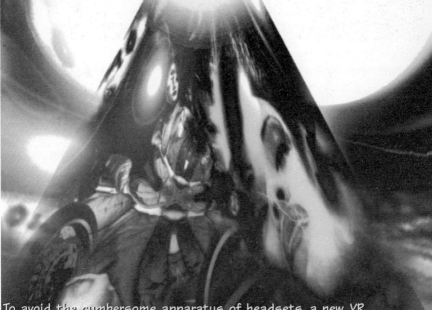

To avoid the cumbersome apparatus of headsets, a new VR development is the 'cave' which uses a pointer, worn by one person who acts as guide for a small group, in a dome or room on which stereo images or the virtual reality are back-projected.

Which computer?

 A book like this cannot tell you which machine is best for you. It can only help you feel more confident to make choices about connecting with cyberspace.

The best advice we can offer is this:

Think hard about whether you really want a computer and, if you do, why?

If you don't really need one, wait until you do ... and spend your money on something you really do want!

If you do want a computer, make a list of what you need it for: essentials, preferences and what you don't want. Then do some research.

Try out other people's machines & programmes and find the ones you like.

Which operating system do you prefer?

Just want to play games?

Want a CD-ROM?

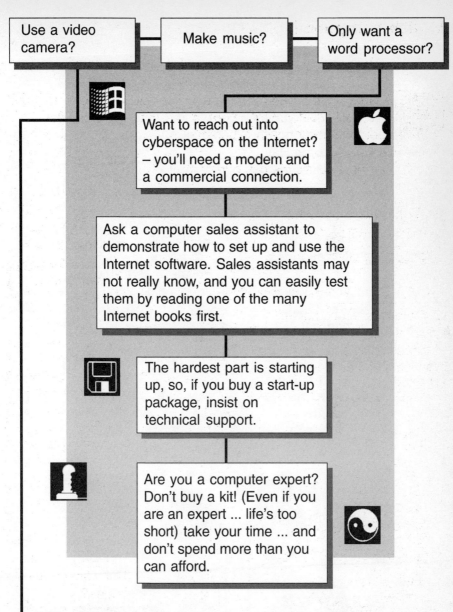

Use a video camera?

Make music?

Only want a word processor?

Want to reach out into cyberspace on the Internet? – you'll need a modem and a commercial connection.

Ask a computer sales assistant to demonstrate how to set up and use the Internet software. Sales assistants may not really know, and you can easily test them by reading one of the many Internet books first.

The hardest part is starting up, so, if you buy a start-up package, insist on technical support.

Are you a computer expert? Don't buy a kit! (Even if you are an expert ... life's too short) take your time ... and don't spend more than you can afford.

Computer speeds and processing capacities are at least doubling every year. By the time you've exhausted the possibilities of your first machine, you'll be in a position to make the most of incredible possibilities. In a few years, you will voyage further into uncharted cyberspace than you or I can currently imagine!

Global communications systems

The balance of power in communications systems is shifting from passively received broadcast media to participatory networks.

The BBC radio World Service, although still influential, is being overtaken by global cable channels like CNN and MTV.

Amateur 'ham' and CB radio networks have Internet equivalents. Broadcast Net radio stations carrying news, music and BBSs allow for inter-communication between individuals and news providers. Anyone on the Internet can broadcast video using the Mbone facility.

The ISDN networks are capable of almost infinite bandwidth, allowing everyone to broadcast their own messages and receive hundreds of other people's ideas, all the time, at very little cost.

Satellite and cable TV systems are frequently used as private links for business, sport, religion and politics, as well as carrying telephone and computer network services.

Cell phone companies permit calls from any place on Earth to any other, with possible Internet dial-up connections from bath-tubs to beaches.

The zenith of the electronic information market-place is the Internet.

Video conferencing

The term Video Conferencing is used to describe a simultaneous
communication of several people in different locations,
where each person sits in front of a TV camera and sees
the others on their monitors.

New technology allows different type of signals to be sent along the
single telephone line simultaneously. It is possible to connect a
computer to such a line and have concurrent audio, video and data
communication with several people at the same time. Each user can
divide their computer screen into several parts to be able to see the
others and study the data almost as they would in reality.
This type of communication enables a microsurgeon to perform an
operation on a patient hundreds of miles away, or a big multinational
company to put up the price of bread througout the world.

Only connect

 Although most of us have only recently become aware of the Internet, this year is its 25th anniversary.

It all started in the 1960s with the ARPANET (Advanced Research Project Agency Network) built by the US Defense Department, connecting computers to radio and satellite systems to support military research into networks that would still work even if part was destroyed in wartime.

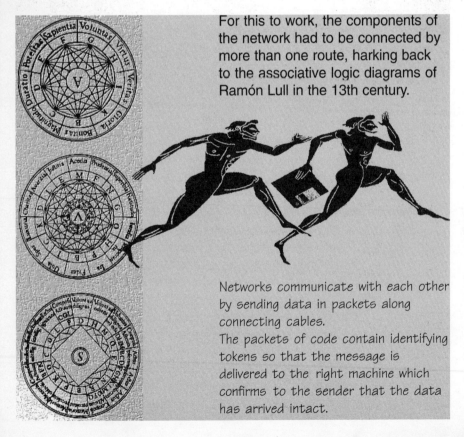

For this to work, the components of the network had to be connected by more than one route, harking back to the associative logic diagrams of Ramón Lull in the 13th century.

Networks communicate with each other by sending data in packets along connecting cables.
The packets of code contain identifying tokens so that the message is delivered to the right machine which confirms to the sender that the data has arrived intact.

Correct addressing on the Internet uses the Internet Protocol (IP) and enables any computer using any operating system to communicate with any other, almost! This arrangement was arrived at during the development of networking software in the USA, UK and Scandinavia as local area networks (LAN).

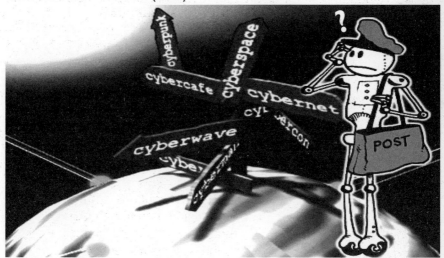

LANs in private company offices used work stations connected to a central computer. All these terminals could talk to each other because they use the same main CPU.
To make sure that IP packages all reached their destination, the Transmission Control Protocol (TCP) labels each packet and counts them all in at the receiving end. Wide Area Networks (WANs) are exactly the same, but spread over long distances.

The US National Science Foundation built its own network (NSFnet) using IP technology. This connected main centres across the USA with local chains around each node. This system was upgraded in 1987, demonstrating the beauty of the original concept of the ARPANET. Because of multiple interconnections, repairs and upgrading go unnoticed since the network automatically finds alternative routes of transmission.
This mode of connectivity is called **rhizomatic** from rhizome, the underground rootlike stem of some plants, the roots and shoots of which are both separate and collective.
The NSFnet joined the ARPANET, and the Internet began.

IBM, AMEX and EXXON have had their own private networks for many years before joining the Internet, but now educational establishments from primary schools to research institutes are connected,

as well as private individuals, commercial outlets and even Bill Clinton.

News on every subject, bulletin boards for groups with similar interests, and simple electronic mail (e-mail) are all available. There's something for everyone...

Technical terms on any subject tend to induce technophobia. Don't worry, it's very simple really...

TCP/IP are the sending and receiving protocols that make sure that messages get through to log in to a remote computer. For example, to use a database, software called Telnet is used – an applications programme just like any other. Once you have logged in with Telnet, the very complex software translates between your machine, the designated client, because you request the services and the remote computer the server, since it supplies the services.

FTP allows you to exchange files between the client and server.

Unless these are 'Anonymous FTP' files with free access, you may need a password to do this. E-mail is the simplest software on the Net and used most for simple correspondence.

Every message can be sent to any number of machines with no extra cost or effort, permitting multiple mailshots and Bulletin Board Systems (BBSs) or newsgroups where real-time group discussion on every subject takes place, for example 'alt.cyberspace'!

President Clinton's e-mail address looks like this: president@whitehouse.gov

Addresses used to be numeric but were hard to remember ... now every Internet user has a mail box with their name or nickname at (@) a particular machine (whitehouse) in some category (gov).

Countries outside the USA also have a country suffix, e.g. .uk, .de (for Germany).

There is so much information in so many places on the Internet that software to search on particular topics is essential. Archie searches Internet servers, Gopher goes and gets information.

The greatest innovation of the 90s, the path to cyberspace, is the hypertext GUI.

Mosaic and World Wide Web (WWW) will conduct searches of both text and pictures and present sound and video within hypertext pages.
The Internet video telephone facility, Mbone, works with these interfaces.

Mosaic and WWW are increasing access to the net because they are so easy to use.

Categories include .edu(cation), .ac(ademic), .co(mmercial), .mil(itary) or .org(anization).

Infobahn

 Everyone is equal on the Net, but some are more equal than others.

Major players in its development in the United States will have international effects.

U.S.Vice President Al Gore is credited with having coined the term 'Information Superhighway'. He advocates introduction of a standard encryption device, the Clipper chip, alongside the limiting of private encryption in an attempt to thwart criminal use of the Internet.

Esther Dyson:
the Net can 'overcome the economies of scale ... so the big guys don't rule'.

William Gibson doubts that the immediate future of the Infobahn will be anything more than a shopping mall, a mediocre perversion of his original vision.

Bill Gates, founder and chairman of Microsoft and widely thought of as the stereotypical computer nerd, the contemporary 'train spotter', is one of the world's richest and most powerful men.

The Electronic Frontier Foundation (**EFF**) began as an ad hoc group protesting against secret service infiltration of an Internet BBS.
They now find themselves in the position of defending civil rights in cyberspace as a lobbying group with an annual budget of around $1.5m.
Ranging from technology multi - millionaires and an ex - member of the Grateful Dead to one of the original LSD-using Merry Pranksters. EFF members have a common vision of the Internet as a means to individual and collective political action.

Microsoft produces the most widely used operating systems and is set to produce user-friendly software for the Internet, enabling everybody and his dog to get on-line.

'nothing, nowhere, never, unless it is important'
Nicholas Negroponte
nicholas@media.mit.edu
'Just because bandwidth exists, don't squirt more bits at me'
info grazing, channel surfing...

Gates claims that his products will have no influence on future society, that the content of the 'Infosphere' will be more influential than the Net itself. Marshall McLuhan would disagree. Bill Gates' book **The Road Ahead** will describe the future as he sees it...

With entire news journals taking only seconds to reach you, Negroponte recommends using 'interface agents' to select personalized information from the torrent pounding at your terminal: the 'Daily Me'.

> 'Knowledge dwells
> In heads replete with thoughts of other men;
> Wisdom in minds attentive to their own'
> William Cowper

Start browsing!

 The Internet isn't just email, but its a great start.

Write notes to friends and relatives near and far – its good to talk.
esperanto@rand.org

Find and download information on your favourite stars and subjects.
ftp eff.org:/pub/EFF/
ftp std.com:/obi/Tennyson
ftp explorer.arc.nasa.gov
ftp newton.newton..cam.ac.uk

Join Usenet groups and BBSs. Read the FAQ (frequently asked questions), get involved in the discussion, join Internet Relay Chat (IRC) groups for real-time debate.

Talk to people in every country of the world, practise your foreign languages, discuss great literature and science, swap recipes and stories, make friends and influence people ...

If you want to change the world do it by example and persuasion ... join in, don't censor (give yourself a chance to learn what other people like).

alt.alien.visitors

alt.binaries.pictures.erotica

alt.binaries.pictures.erotica.blondes

alt.binaries.pictures.erotica.male
alt.bonsai
alt.comedy.british
alt.devilbunnies
alt.drugs.caffeine
alt.evil
alt.misc.forsale
alt.personals
alt.radio.pirate
alt.rave

alt.sex.bondage.particle.physics
alt.sex.pictures
alt.wired
alt.zines
rec.autos

rec.games.mud.announce
rec.games.mud.misc
rec.gardens
rec.pets.dogs
rec.pets.cats
rec.crafts.misc
rec.music.classical
rec.music.celtic
sci.anthropology
sci.bio.ecology
sci.classics

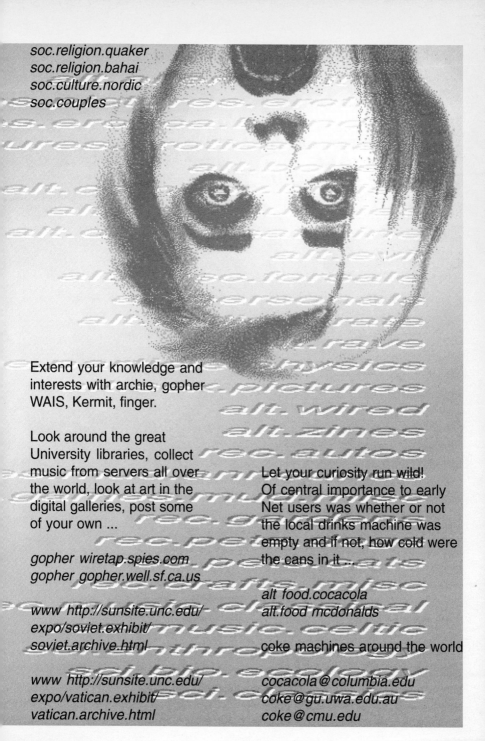

soc.religion.quaker
soc.religion.bahai
soc.culture.nordic
soc.couples

Extend your knowledge and
interests with archie, gopher
WAIS, Kermit, finger.

Look around the great
University libraries, collect
music from servers all over
the world, look at art in the
digital galleries, post some
of your own ...

gopher wiretap.spies.com
gopher gopher.well.sf.ca.us

www http://sunsite.unc.edu/
expo/soviet.exhibit/
soviet.archive.html

www http://sunsite.unc.edu/
expo/vatican.exhibit/
vatican.archive.html

Let your curiosity run wild!
Of central importance to early
Net users was whether or not
the local drinks machine was
empty and if not, how cold were
the cans in it ...

alt food.cocacola
alt.food mcdonalds

coke machines around the world

cocacola@columbia.edu
coke@gu.uwa.edu.au
coke@cmu.edu

Money makes the world go round

 That is why calculating machines were first developed. Remember Pascal?

International finance is big business.

Stock exchanges dealing in national and international shares and currencies constantly publish exchange rates and indexes of market trading.

Markets in shares and futures and the banking and clearing system would be impossible without the sophisticated telecommunications and computing systems connecting the world banks and the treasuries of the world's governments.

Innovations in banking are beginning to incorporate telephone and Internet connections.

Personal banking can now be done almost entirely by phone. Smart cards instantly transmit transaction information to central computers and record account details.
Miniature computers built into the card are replacing credit and debit cards.

Payment for Internet services by credit card will gradually be replaced by direct bank exchanges. 'Electronic money' need never be seen or printed. Paper currency and coinage is very expensive to produce and worthless in itself, only valuable for what it represents.

Hacking into financial computer networks can be very profitable, although modern security procedures are trying to make this impossible.

There is a story of a bank employee who wrote a computer program to deduct any amount the bank would normally round down to the nearest currency unit, 0.4p in the UK, (or 0.4 cents if the story is set in the USA) from every account for which interest was calculated.

This is a very small amount on its own, but within months, so the story goes, the inventive employee had accumulated millions of pounds because so many similar calculations are performed every day.

Remote banking tends to encourage fraud.

From the days when your word was your bond, through legal recognition of the handshake and the signature, we have come to a point where our password or 4-digit PIN (personal identification number) is the only way to gain access to what we own. And a 4-digit code is fairly easy to crack!

The effect of computing on commerce and industry has been profound.

Henry Ford started a trend for de-skilling, in the name of efficiency, through the principle of the assembly-line division of labour.

Computer-controlled robots have replaced people on production lines in every area of manufacturing.

Although computerization has reduced the need for unskilled workers and removed much of the job satisfaction of those who remain, in skilled professions the new trend is towards multi-skilling and multi-tasking.

Recognition of improved productivity and quality of work from employees who follow a job from start to finish is changing the working environment for those still in employment. Computers are revolutionizing many industries, from publishing (CD-ROM) to retail (home shopping and direct marketing).

Market research using clever software modelling and accurate databases can pinpoint consumers more accurately.

Mailshots of the future will come via Internet and cable TV. The production and distribution of goods is also computerized.

Stock control and distribution is becoming almost automatic in response to point-of-sales statistics produced by computerized tills.

Weather

 Weather costs money. The construction, farming, airlines, shipping, entertainment and insurance industries depend on good weather. This encourages investment in forecasting.

The resolution of satellite images from the outer atmosphere is so good that car number-plates can be identified. Data from these sources are compiled by computer and used to model weather systems.

Detection and prediction of weather all over the world is a massive enterprise, using data from satellites, balloons, ships, aircraft, radar, land stations and buoys, many of which operate automatically.

Recent computer-generated mathematical contributions to weather prediction – fractals and chaos theory – have advanced our understanding of both the development of weather systems and of geology.

Satellites and reconnaissance aircraft are often dual-purpose, collecting military information as well as weather data.

The unity and interdependence of every aspect of the world is beautifully illustrated by the butterfly effect.

Hey, flapping our wings here may cause a hurricane in China!

Yeah! Boot up and let's flap!

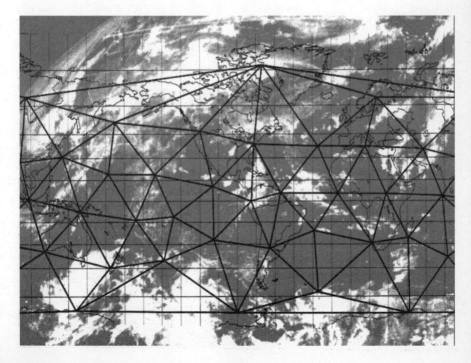

The science of weather, meteorology, although inexact, is something of a luxury – rich countries can afford better information than poorer ones.

It is also a political issue – global warming, the ozone layer and pollution are meteorological hot potatoes.

In sickness and in health ...

 Modern hospitals have come to rely on computerized technology. From scanners and pacemakers to sample analysis and patient records, medicine is now high-tech.

Although the human brain is infinitely more complex than any computer, we benefit from every aspect of the microprocessor.

Microsurgery techniques use computer-enhanced imaging, video and fibre optics. Surgeons are trained to use 3D and VR simulators. The pharmaceutical industry is creating new compounds and materials with nano-engineering technology.

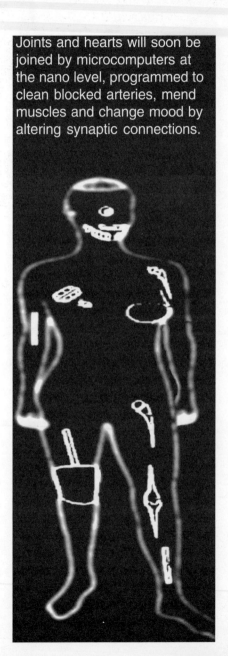

Joints and hearts will soon be joined by microcomputers at the nano level, programmed to clean blocked arteries, mend muscles and change mood by altering synaptic connections.

(Nano is a size description like kilo and mega, of 10^{-9}. One thousand millionth.)

The language of medicine is increasingly military, talking of 'invasion', 'fighting cancer' and 'combating depression'.

Video conferencing is already used for diagnosis and prescription by distant specialists.

Although obviously cheaper and easier than employing more consultants, this eliminates human contact between doctor and patient.

Research has shown that bedside manner is an important part of a cure!

Till death do us part

 ENIAC just missed being used to crack communication codes in the Second World War, but since then computers have become essential in warfare.

From databases of intelligence gathered by agents and surveillance devices to control of war machines and missiles, computers appear as mainframe controlling and modelling aids, networked machines and dedicated hardware.

Phone-tapping and high resolution satellite imaging detect and track vehicles, conversations and individuals.

GCHQ in the UK monitors thousands of telephone calls simultaneously, using sound pattern recognition technology.

The Gulf War of 1992 in Kuwait and Iraq was controlled by intelligent machines. Pilots previously trained in simulators with 'head-up' displays matching a mapped and modelled virtual landscape of Iraq.

This was the first 'virtual war', analyzed by the post-modern theorist Jean Baudrillard.

Strikes and battles seemed timed to coincide with US news bulletins.

Terrain-following, heat-seeking and remotely guided missiles, some with video cameras used for TV coverage, were controlled by computerized Command Systems.

The Command Control also received information about all its own vehicles and aircraft, preventing them from being mistaken for targets.

British aircraft were nevertheless shot down, which demonstrates the fallibility even of this extremely sophisticated machinery.

Human error is just as likely.

One of the terrifying fantasies of the 1980s was President Reagan's Star Wars, a hugely expensive 'off world' demonstration of technological superiority, a logical extension of weapons research which adopts as a priority the protection of commercial interests above human life.

This scenario and the possibilities for abuse were beautifully described in Vernor Vinge's novella **True Names**, anticipating Gibson's cyberspace by a couple of years.

BUTLER

BOMB

Work, rest and play

Most computing in schools and universities involves increasing access to libraries, galleries, databases etc., rather than studying computing.

Educational theory suggests that interactivity is the basis of learning.

The traditional 'broadcast' approach of transmitting facts from teacher to pupil is being replaced by education at the learner's pace, each student choosing his or her own path through a curriculum.

The division between education and recreation, always arbitrary and restrictive, is at last being broken down.

Until interactivity was sufficiently developed in the early 1970s, computer games were slow and largely intellectual.

One of the first tests of machine intelligence was the chess-playing computer, ideal for solo games over long periods of time.

The computerization of **Dungeons and Dragons**, a text-based role-playing game, widened the audience of game players, but excitement and adrenaline is more saleable, so commercial research concentrated on real-time interactivity.

Tetris, a simple but testing computer game designed by a Russian, has become the most popular game yet designed.

Score:
15777
Level:
8
Lines:
70

The first commercial computer games appeared in the 1970s with 'space invaders' and simple tennis-like scenarios.
A new industry quickly emerged selling dedicated computers for video-games, attached to the TV like a video recorder.
Early domestic computers were almost all bought for games.

Personal computers used for other purposes can also be used for games, now available on tape, disc and CD-ROM.

Small, battery-powered game machines took computers on to the street around the same time as portable telephones.

Doom quote: 'Knee deep in the dead!'

Multi-media systems of the 1990s have become what the music centre was to the 1970s.

Sports games such as golf and tennis claim to improve the player's real game through hand-to-eye coordination!

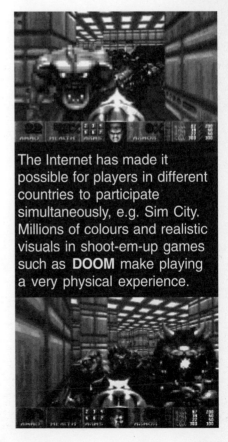

The Internet has made it possible for players in different countries to participate simultaneously, e.g. Sim City. Millions of colours and realistic visuals in shoot-em-up games such as **DOOM** make playing a very physical experience.

The game structure of Dungeons & Dragons was transferred to multi-user dungeons (MUDs and MOOs–Object-Oriented MUDs). MUD participants create a character by typing text descriptions of appearance and behaviour into the communal 'space' of the on-line dungeon.

Other players have no way of knowing if the character corresponds to the real body or personality of the player. It is assumed that all players are male, whatever gender their avatar possesses, because so many men present a female alter ego.

Realism and interactivity in computer games are using advances in military and aerospace interface research, particularly virtual reality.

In the 21st century, it will be possible to pick your volleyball team from every willing on-line player and play in a global league.

The main advantage of VR interactivity is the possibility of physical participation, getting away from the body-numbing seat in front of a keyboard and screen.

Jacking-in to cyberspace will introduce new games, both mental and physical, using invented bodies in fantastical worlds.

Politics

X The use of computers in politics, minimal until the 1950s, became invaluable in modelling the behaviours of populations of people, transport, education and health needs.

Television is the government's mainline communication with the electorate.
Political broadcasting, like tele-evangelism, is a genre in itself.

The lengthy intellectual debates of the 19th century have given way to the sound-bite. Appearance and sex appeal, have triumphed over policy in elections.

The introduction of interactive TV, enabling instant referenda on every possible debate, is unlikely to enhance democracy. Enfranchisement would become an issue of **who** has access to technology.

IF VOTING MADE ANY DIFFERENCE, THEY'D ABOLISH IT!

TELL US!
THEY
WHAT
KNOW
WE ONLY

The onus for acquiring relevant information would rest heavily with the voter.

Voting on sensitive issues, about which most people would be unable to make informed decisions, would become very susceptible to pressure-group politics.

An optimist might see this as a welcome form of anarchy, but the diminishing responsibility of elected representatives in central government does not reduce its power or control.

History is not a single truth. It is written by those in power.

So many people feeding on information from the same sources makes manipulation of population easy.
When unpalatable facts give way to a good story, we get **virtual history**.

Crime

Early photofit pictures and artists' impressions generated amusing and unrecognizable images. Modern software has made the 'wanted' pictures more realistic but unreliable for identification purposes.

Fingerprint matching has been computerized for twenty years. Methods of pattern analysis have become much more sophisticated.

Key features are coded and stored in databases which can be accessed by international police forces.

Here doc, take it! I need new fingerprints, new face and some DNA – FAST!

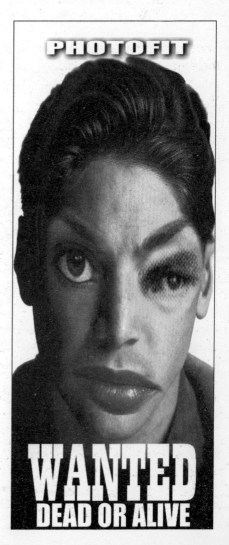

Hey guys, where do I file this?

DNA type-matching can identify 1 person in 10,000, considered by some juries to be insufficiently certain for conviction.

When the Genome Project is complete, a much higher rate of accuracy in DNA matching will be possible, approaching 100%.

The Internet has been used by international crime syndicates since the early days. Mafia, Yakuza and Triads are pooling their resources and creating a 'smart crime' fast lane on the Information Superhighway.

Money-laundering, shifting balances through accounts so that its origins can't be traced, is a predominant activity of computer criminals.

Criminal hackers work full-time to break security codes and gain entry to valuable information held in financial and state computers.

Civil liberties and security

X Civil liberties and security become extremely important when databases containing all kinds of information about everyone in the world become part of a universally accessible network.

A clever hacker lucky enough to discover passwords into classified computer documents could steal your money, blackmail you, alter personal documents or simply create mischief!

Many brilliant computer hackers in the 1980s were offered employment in government agencies trying to develop security systems.

Stories abound of teenage boys breaking into banks, CIA mainframes and military control equipment. Free telephone calls have been relatively easy to achieve with the right gizmos, called 'blue boxes' in the USA.

Criminal use of coded messages on the Internet has led to calls for universal encryption devices.

In the USA, the authorities are advocating the installation of the Clipper Chip in every modem or network connection.

This microchip would encode all communications sent and received, assuring privacy, except from the CIA.

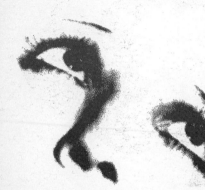

Holding the key to encryption, they would be able to track illegal transactions. This assumes that criminals are incapable of using alternative encryption methods and that universal surveillance is acceptable to all Internet users.

The authorities are resisting use of completely impenetrable encryption software that they would not be able to monitor.

Every time a connection into cyberspace is made information travels in both directions. Not only do you, the cybersurfer, meet your friends in a MUD, explore the Bodleian library in Oxford, the Australian patent office, or buy a few items from the on-line shopping mall – they find out about **you**.

Your computer identifies itself at each connection. Your financial details are recorded every time you pay for goods or information. Your consumer profile becomes more detailed, enabling direct mailing companies to locate you.

Civil liberties organizations see this as an extension of state power and advise use of additional technology which could give a degree of anonymity.

LET US CONTROL YOU!

The former 'Iron Curtain' countries have enormous expertise but little hardware and investment.

Many famous computer viruses have emerged from Bulgaria, programmers apparently having no real work to keep them occupied!

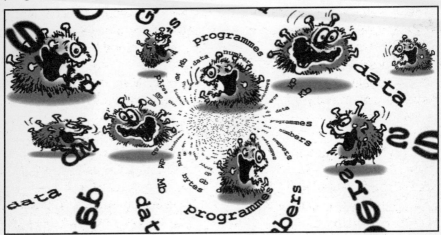

A plague of viruses transmitted on software discs in the 1980s caused havoc in thousands of personal computers.
Virus-detecting software can eradicate old infections but cannot anticipate new ones. Infection via the Internet could cause massive damage.

Payments for information in the form of writing, pictures, music and designs depend on copyright.
One expects to have to pay for other people's work, but there is also a feeling that information should be free, and freely available.

Current litigation will determine new copyright law on the Internet.

Multimedia

 Information is passing to consumerism.

Cross-referencing and indexes make the use of encyclopedias and reference books easy.

Ted Nelson invented the term hypertext in the 1960s to describe an interactive programme providing multiple pathways through text or images via cross-referenced or related content.

Multimedia includes text, sound, images, animation, video and interactive 3D environments, all in the same package.

The connections between items and sequences can be programmed into the multimedia or requested by the user in the form of word or date associations.

Readers choose their own paths through the hypertext options, creating unique combinations and sequences not experienced by other readers or by the author.

Traditional linear media, such as books or films, display their creator's art and skill and in content structure, presentation and control of an audience over time.

Multimedia calls for the author to relinquish control to the consumer – a shift to participatory art forms.

A universal desire for heroes, masthead figures and stories suggests that the artist will always be needed, if only to produce soap operas.

Truth and beauty are part of the human condition and are reflected in the technology of the age.

Cyber-art is already being made.
VR art and electronic images appear in galleries on the Internet, USENET groups share stories and poems, musicians collaborate on compositions and dancers have created computer choreography for both humans and virtual bodies.

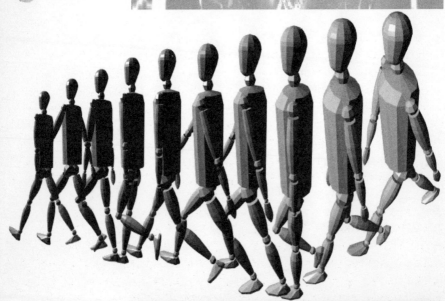

Short attention span, instant gratification, fragmented knowledge ... can this possibly generate wisdom?

Heralded as the Gutenberg revolution of the 20th century, multimedia encyclopedias are available as hypermedia in the home on CD-ROM, or via the Internet, giving access to the world's libraries and museums.

As it becomes more apparent that knowledge is power and that education does not happen only at school, personal computers with multimedia facilities are advertised as family resources.

Edutainment and **infotainment** are the buzzwords of the 90s.

The CD-ROM is now not only a new way to sell music, it's the medium of encyclopedias, financial management, games, art galleries, museums, cookery courses and films!

The domestic multimedia technologies are often supplied with a modem, allowing even more access to entertainment and reference material via other computers worldwide.

It's a staggering thought that to put all this information on the Internet means the conversion of all knowledge into binary!
But is this knowledge?
What about scholarship?

The revolution

 The revolution in information technology changed the ways we work and communicate.

Hard copy on paper and 3D constructions have given way to soft copy stored in computer memory. Information is created, stored and transmitted without ever existing as anything other than 0s and 1s, shown as light on a screen.

A major effect of technology on employment was the production-line robot.

The next big leap has already begun. Many service and light manufacturing industries have traditionally employed home-workers.
Internet connections make it possible for all computing, communications and design businesses to do the same.

CRT monitors are hard on the eyes and not very easily portable. Laptop computers with liquid crystal screens, although useful, are expensive and not always convenient. No doubt someone will invent a small 'book' device for reading in the bath.

The paperless office was welcomed by computer pioneers as a 'greener' way to work.
In fact the computer revolution has generated more paper in the form of print-out than was ever used before – people like paper.

Officeless maybe, but definitely not paperless!

Telematics, homeworking using computer connection, will have an enormous effect on peoples' lives.

Its advantages are that travel and office costs are reduced, travel time is zero, communication is efficient on-line and employees can work at their own rate.

The down-side is that people will be alone all day, removing the social aspects of going to work. Stimulating conversation at the workplace, which has often led to innovation in the task, will be lost. Employment will probably become part-time and less secure.
Evidence that homeworking improves efficiency, because workers are interrupted less and feel guilty when they take a break, is encouraging to businesses suitable for telematics.

It has just come to our attention that you have used up all your tea-breaks until the year 2009!

Computer homeworkers often keep videophone connections of their friends on-screen so that they can chat occasionally.

We'll see ...

Artificial intelligence

The word **robot**, (from the Czech *robota,* 'forced labour'), was first used by Karel Capek in the 1920s to describe an artificial man.

In his **Discourse on Method** in 1637, Descartes conceived of a machine that could 'utter words' or 'cry that it was hurt'.
He only knew of clockwork figures, primitive when compared with modern computers, but he conjectured that, however clever the machine, it would never be able to hold a conversation with a human being.

Human conversation was also the basis of the test devised by **Alan Turing** (the English mathematician whose brilliant analytical mind helped crack the German's Enigma code in WW2), in the 1930s to frame research into artificial intelligence.

To separate factors of appearance, voice and character from intelligence, a person holds a conversation via computer keyboard and screen. If the human subject believes the answers to be human, then the computer has passed the **Turing** test.
A machine passing this test may be assumed to be capable of other less complex tasks, but it may only be good at having conversations!

Mimicry of human thought-processes requires a vast database and extremely complex programming, but is not creatively intelligent in the way people (or some animals) are.

Even expert systems and software that learn from experience aren't capable of the paradigm shifts that transform data into knowledge or experience into wisdom.

All enthusiasts would probably disagree ...

Artificial life

Langton's ants were an innovation in computer software breeding new 'life-forms' from given parameters, just as DNA produces infinite variety in living creatures. Self-reproducing systems such as these are leading research to create a fifth generation of computers which will learn, repair themselves and evolve new programs in a fraction of the time people could write them.

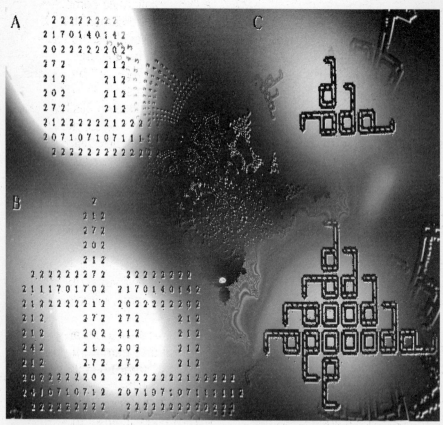

We are used to 'top-down' structures that echo feudal systems in management chains of command. From the increasing use of 'bottom-up' learning systems it would seem that anarchy may have it's uses!

Cyborgs

 Cyborg is a contraction of 'cybernetic organism', first used in 1960 by Manfred Clynes. It describes the hybrid of human and machine, simultaneously biological and technological, which results from procedures in biomedical engineering.

Surgical implants of mechanical devices – plastic hip joints, mechanical hearts or pacemakers – produces cyborgs. Microelectronics and miniaturisation have enabled modern medicine to repair and replace dysfunctional biology.

This dependence of the human on the machine can be seen as symbiosis between human and machine. The boundary between the 'natural' and the artificial is dissolving. We have been cyborgs since humans first used tools.

Examples of man (or woman) and machine operating together in perfect synchrony are routine, car drivers being an obvious example.

Mechanical control of human beings by machines and computers in particular have been themes in myth and literature for centuries.

Science fantasy creatures from **Frankenstein** to the replicants of **Blade Runner** address the question of balance between invasive technology and the human. For the 'Bionic Man', the technology was benign, an asset – a demonstration that technology isn't inherently evil.

Frankenstein's monster was a misunderstood creation of man.

What kind of class or caste system will evolve to denote the purely human, the controllable cyborg drone and all the grades in between?

These are questions of free will, identity, autonomy and constraint.

The busiest Usenet groups on the Internet seem to be about sex: alt.sex.cyberspace carries discussion on cyberotics and the possibility of the cyborgasm by mental stimulation while jacked-in to a neural interface. This may seem trivial, but a great deal of research into sensory interfaces is driven by commercial interests that see enormous potential in a virtual sex industry.

Cyberfeminists claim the Internet as an uncharted, ungendered territory in which representation of the self is inevitably androgynous.

It is impossible to be sure of the sex of any one in cyberspace, an ideal opportunity to forget inhibitions and prejudices and concentrate on what people say, who they really are.

In the absence of any uncharted territory remaining on Earth (and with the exploration of space proving too expensive and taking too long) restless and enquiring minds turned first to psychology, the exploration of the mind and soul.

Cyberia is the territory for a collective psychology, its shape and size limited only by human desire and imagination.
It is not a world 'out there' to conquer and subdue, but an electronically assisted, unlimited collective mind.

The Internet is ripe for exploitation. Businesses everywhere are searching for ways of cashing in.

In the next few years, the number of computers connected to it is expected to grow exponentially, exceeding over 100 million across the world by the end of the millennium. And for each computer there are likely to be several users.

Advertisers are looking for ways of reaching the largest market ever realizable, without incurring the wrath of MUD wizards and electronic warriors who defend the liberty and access of the citizens of Cyberia.

Junk mail is not well received.

An entrepreneurial salesman sending blanket email to the whole US network was flamed out of existence, effectively disconnected, by angry sys-ops who resented having their computers, extensions of themselves, invaded by commercial interests.

Civil rights in cyberspace are gradually being formulated among cyberian communities who find themselves obliged to deal with such transgression.

In any ad hoc community exploring and settling in a new world, rules are agreed and law enforcers emerge.

The Electronic Frontier Foundation, a collection of the old hands and figureheads of the Internet, has formed to take on the US government over the issues of security and secrecy.

The New York magazine **Village Voice** carried a report of 'A Rape in Cyberspace'.

A female MUD character was made to 'speak' and 'act' in uncharacteristic and unpleasant ways by another participant. The victim claimed to have felt as violated and abused as in any physical situation where one's behaviour and speech are controlled by another person. After several (on-line) meetings of the 'elders' of this community, the wizard was persuaded to exile the perpetrator of the virtual 'crime'.

Cyberspace communities are as protective of their members as any group of friends or neighbours in 'real' life.

They probably have more in common than most physical groups since their allegiance is intellectual rather than based on proximity.

Externally applied rules and regulations will be vigorously resisted by the early settlers who feel they have found and begun to explore the first great electronic wilderness.

'The net sees censorship as damage and routes around it.'

A state of sublime ecstasy

 Cyberspace as envisaged by Gibson involves constant drug use in conjunction with a collective neural network.

International dance music, with a pulsing, hypnotic rhythm of around 130 bpm (beats per minute!), is enhanced by the use of 'smart' foods and drinks containing natural stimulants.

Lasers, smoke, strobes and projected fantastical images produce a hypnotic state of sublime ecstasy!

Referred to as E, the synthetic neural stimulant MDMA or Ecstasy was first made illegal in the mid 1980s, several years after it became a popular recreational drug.

Cyberspace is essentially about communication in any way possible, the important thing being the exchange of ideas, electronically or actively in the dance.

Originally used in psychotherapy and mystic ceremonies, it is now only legally available in Switzerland where a few psychiatrists prescribe it for depression.

Turn on, tune in, boot up!

Cynics suggest that E is tacitly accepted by the authorities because docile young people are less challenging to the establishment than aware and disenchanted ones.

But cyberspace community and cooperation might lead to political consciousness of a new kind.

Similar (r)evolutionary effects were claimed for LSD in the 60s and are now being claimed for MDMA and its very potent alternative, DMT.

Leary and McKenna consider that psychotropic drugs and inter-brain connection are part of the same mind expanding project.

Timothy Leary, LSD guru of the 1960s, has also become an influential figure in the story of cyberspace.

Along with Terence McKenna, the equivalent figure for 1990s drug culture, he believes that the quantum leap of human language came about through the accidental use of psychotropic foods.

Yes, and you may end up a zapped-out, brain-dead cyberzombie!

Seeing the shape

 The three great technological revolutions have each had to do with **information**:

1 The **Gutenberg Revolution** increased access to and dissemination of knowledge.

2 The **Industrial Revolution** speeded up both acquisition and exchange of information.

3 And the **Information Revolution** is dramatically changing the status of knowledge and the status of people too.

The key to this change is **control**.

Feedback systems free us from the control of machines and make those machines more efficient and precise.

The control of information by our powerful and ubiquitous computers can feed the paranoia of those without power, but computers can also make power more widely available as information is released into the world via the Internet. Industry and science are more creative when people get involved. Management structures are shifting towards the model of Lao-Tzu, a Chinese sage of the 6th century BC, whose words could apply to cyberspace:

Intelligent control appears as <u>uncontrol</u> or freedom.

The 'white hot' technological revolution welcomed in the 1960s has become the information revolution of the 1990s.

The technologies making teleworking, video-conferencing and mass personal communication possible have apparently been superseded in importance by the content they carry.

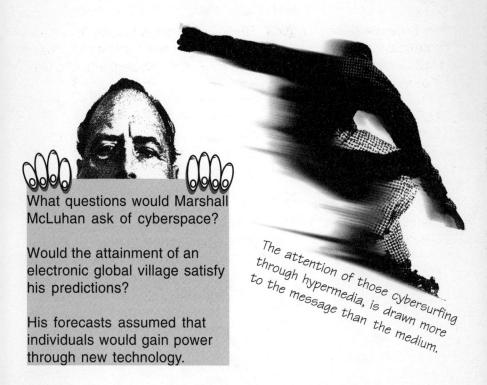

What questions would Marshall McLuhan ask of cyberspace?

Would the attainment of an electronic global village satisfy his predictions?

His forecasts assumed that individuals would gain power through new technology.

The attention of those cybersurfing through hypermedia, is drawn more to the message than the medium.

Electronic extensions of the body, heralded as evidence of the disintegration of the self, subsume the individual and force a new interpretation of McLuhan's 'medium as message'.

If the medium transforms individual subjects into disembodied pulses of information, what is the message?

Perhaps the atomization and idealization of the individual is giving way to a new collective, a metamorphosis of intelligence in which we all engage – a rhizome.

Here's looking at you

 'Big Brother' has always been present in the form of public and secret government agents.

Policing the Internet is a nearly impossible task because there is so much traffic and because identity is easily camouflaged.

Indeed one American sysop provides an anonymity service, stripping all identifiers from messages directed via his server, so that people feel free to express themselves.

Multiple-copying technologies, such as the twelve carbon copies of samizdat and the fax, helped bring down the old Soviet Union and other Iron Curtain powers.

Distribution of information is essential for people to be free.

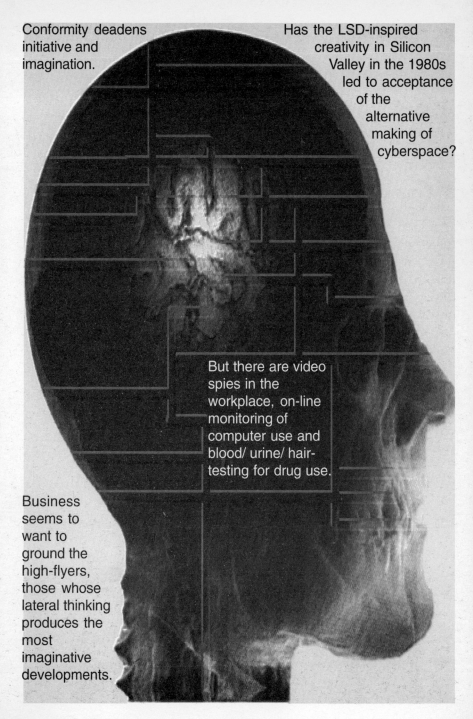

Conformity deadens initiative and imagination.

Has the LSD-inspired creativity in Silicon Valley in the 1980s led to acceptance of the alternative making of cyberspace?

But there are video spies in the workplace, on-line monitoring of computer use and blood/ urine/ hair-testing for drug use.

Business seems to want to ground the high-flyers, those whose lateral thinking produces the most imaginative developments.

The future

 What are some of
the possibilities of
the future?

•   The fifth generation of
computers, with intelligence,
robotics and the capacity to
learn and replicate themselves,
will start another revolution.
If machines that hitherto could
only do as they were told can
then think for themselves, even
within parameters set by us,
every mundane task in the world
could be automated.

Will this free us to do the
'important' things in life?
What will they be?

•   Current genetic
research is aiming to map
the human **genome** within
the next ten years.
The genome is the total of an
organism's genes, in this
case 3 billion base pairs on
100,000 genes on the DNA
of our 46 chromosomes.

The grail of human genetics,
the Human Genome Project,
will identify and lead to cures for
all manner of ailments.

There is concern about the
copyrighting of genomes, even
plans to patent genetic
information discovered during
this research. It will also assist
genetic engineering projects,
exploring cyborg design,
and contribute to the
study of memory.

If all of life's experience is stored
at the genetic level, then one
future fantasy might be to
retrieve it with the assistance of
bio-computers and pass it
on to others.

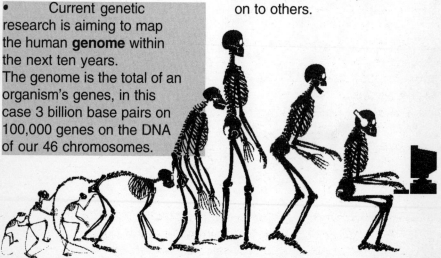

Orwell's warnings of Big Brother in **1984** may have come to pass, who knows?

Gibson himself would welcome living in the Sprawl, his setting for cyberspace, but would you?

Predictions and warnings range from nirvana to a totalitarian or anarchistic hell. It may be naïve to imagine that we can influence the future very much – **the ball has started rolling.**

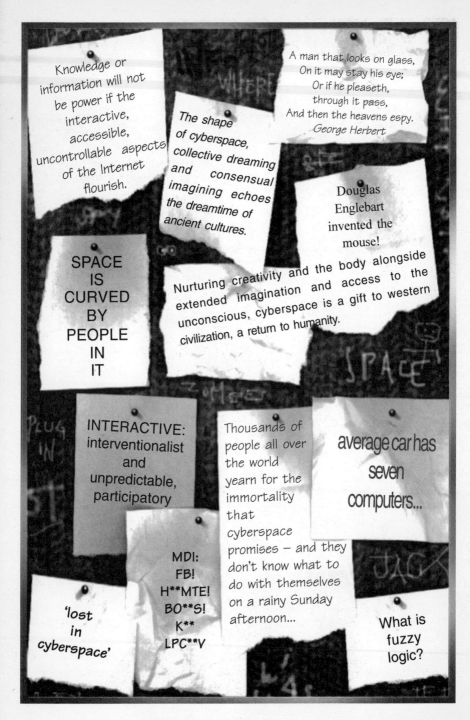

Knowledge or information will not be power if the interactive, accessible, uncontrollable aspects of the Internet flourish.

The shape of cyberspace, collective dreaming and consensual imagining echoes the dreamtime of ancient cultures.

A man that looks on glass,
On it may stay his eye;
Or if he pleaseth,
through it pass,
And then the heavens espy.
George Herbert

Douglas Englebart invented the mouse!

SPACE IS CURVED BY PEOPLE IN IT

Nurturing creativity and the body alongside extended imagination and access to the unconscious, cyberspace is a gift to western civilization, a return to humanity.

INTERACTIVE: interventionalist and unpredictable, participatory

Thousands of people all over the world yearn for the immortality that cyberspace promises – and they don't know what to do with themselves on a rainy Sunday afternoon...

average car has seven computers...

MDI:
FB!
H**MTE!
BO**S!
K**
LPC**V

'lost in cyberspace'

What is fuzzy logic?

We are approaching a time when all knowledge and all ways of manipulating it can be reduced to a string of symbols — is this what we want?

LIMERICK
COUNTY LIBRARY

To find out more ...

General Books

Understanding Media, Marshall McLuhan (MIT, Cambridge, Mass., 1993) For a general introduction to the way technology affects our lives.

The Cyberspace Lexicon, Bob Cotton & Richard Oliver(Phaidon, London, 1994) Wonderful alphabetical asssortment - great stuff!

Cyberia, Douglas Rushkoff (HarperCollins, London, 1994) A tour of the area in the company of certifiable cybernauts.

Cyberspace: First Steps ed. Michael Benedikt (MIT, Cambridge, Mass.,1991) A canter through every aspect with some of the major players.

Virtual Community, Howard Rheingold (Secker, London, 1994) It's all going on now, under your nose!

The Road Ahead, Bill Gates (Viking, London, 1995) Bill's vision...

Chaos & Cyberculture, Timothy Leary (Ronin, Berkeley, 1994) The old dog does new tricks extremely well - and he might be right!

In the Shadow of the Silent Majorities, Jean Baudrillard (Semiotext(e), NewYork 1983) Musing on the effects of the communications explosion.

Computers and the Internet

Computers Simplified, maranGraphics (IDG, San Mateo, 1994) Brilliant intro, all you need.

10 Minute Guide to Buying a Computer, Shelley O'Hara (Alpha, Indianapolis, 1994) If you haven't and you want to, ask a friend or read a book like this.

The Whole Internet, Ed Krol (O'Reilly, Sebastopol, 1994) Friendly, useful and informative, a 'good book'.

Fiction

Neuromancer , William Gibson (Grafton, London, 1986) (etc.) Getting a feel for the future...

Fools , Pat Cadigan (Bantam, New York, 1992) (etc.) Wild virtual body fantasies.

Films

Total Recall with Arnold Schwarzenegger: is it real or is it memory?

Tron : mind games inside the computer.

Lawnmower Man : a good excuse for cybersex.

Magazines

highly recommended for any potential Cyberian are:

Wired (both US and new Euro editions) & **Mondo 2000**: the best Cyberbumf on paper!

New Scientist & **Scientific American:** new technology and thought provocation.

Talk to your nearest computer whizz!

And, of course, the **Internet** itself is at a terminal near you NOW!

Acknowledgements

Joanna would like to thank Jimbo, Richard, Katrine, MCJ, Naomi, John Clancy and Phil Z., dedicated to the Monster, my Mum, and to Gary who took me there.

Zoran is grateful to Spira for keeping the computers alive, to Julia for her time and Maura for her patience. Many thanks to Richard Appignanesi's nerves, Oscar Zarate's help and to my parents for not phoning me too often!

Joanna Buick is a sculptor, photographer and teacher of technology and art. She is currently researching Virtual Reality as a Fine Art Medium at Chelsea College of Art & Design in London.

Zoran Jevtic is an illustrator, heavily involved in computer animation and design, music composition and multimedia. His recent works include: *TLTP* - educational animations, *Storm Over the Balkans* - a book on recent events in former Yugoslavia with Kamenko, and illustrations for *Fantasy Inn Books*.

WITHDRAWN FROM STOCK